Eursule Latiolais, from Catahou... medicine she had was alligator-fat c... but don't get any on your clothes, no ... ...ve throw the clothes away. You can't get rid of the smell," she told me years ago. Now she's 86.

I stopped to visit Eursule on Friday, October 6, 2006, and we got to talking about how the Cajun lifestyle has changed.

"No, but this world is crazy, yeah. I don't mean half crazy, no. I mean CRAZY! The way we live has changed 100%. The way we raise children, too. We're not living the way we did years ago. It's UNREAL. In big cities people used to kill each other, but we didn't have to worry about that around here. Even children are killing other children in schools now.

"We don't get good food anymore. It's all poison. All they know is fertilizer and chemicals. That stuff is everywhere. When they spray crops like sugar cane around here, my plants die. The kids around here all have breathing problems. Meanwhile, we're trying to find healthy food to eat.

"*C'est fou.* Everything is *fou.* It's just crazy everywhere. *Ca vas pas changer, non.* [It won't change] There's no relief in sight."

Greg Guirard

To survive as true Cajuns, we need to continue doing the things for which our culture has always been known, not for the benefit of tourists so much as for our own well-being and spiritual health.

PsychoTherapy for Cajuns

Author, Publisher, Photographer
Greg Guirard

Editing, Proofing and Advice:
Bernie Boudreaux
André Guirard
Janet Faulk
Jean-Paul Guirard

Typing & re-typing: Janet Faulk

Pilot for aerial photos--Ben Seal, Southern Helicopters

Layout: Holly Carruth & Greg Guirard

First Printing: November 2006

ISBN 0-9624778-0-X   978-0-9624778-0-5

Special thanks to the staff at the Center for Louisiana Studies
of the University of Louisiana at Lafayette.

Printed in Canada by the Friesens Corporation

PsychoTherapy
for Cajuns

A Traditional Culture Struggles
for Survival in a Crazy World

Text and Photographs by
Greg Guirard

with

Poetry and Prose by
Sheryl St. Germain

and

Illustrated Poetry by
Sidney Creaghan

and

Illustration on page 58 by
Ben Blanchard

Contents

A Traditional Culture Struggles for Survival in a Crazy World

Several years ago I read a book titled *We've Had 100 Years of Psycho-analysis, and the World Is Getting Worse*, by James Hillman and Michael Ventura. The main theme of the book was this: If for various reasons an individual or group of individuals finds it difficult or impossible to adjust to the values, expectations, and lifestyle of the society as a whole, we must not necessarily assume that there is something wrong with that individual or group of individuals. It is just as likely that the society itself is unbalanced and basically dysfunctional, if not fundamentally insane.

~

I walked into Harold and Myrtle Bigler's home on the main channel of the river one day and noticed that their battery-powered TV was not there.

"Where's your TV, Harold?" I asked.

"I threw the damn' thing in the river," he said. " It's too **crazy** out there."

~

Annie Blanchard was born on a houseboat in the Atchafalaya Basin in 1947. Years ago she told me this: "If you look back on it, people would call you poor.... but we never knew the feeling of being poor. We had everything we needed........ Money don't make you happy. Money just makes you **crazy**."

~

Ten years before she died at her little house in the Basin, Myrtle Bigler told me, "Some people think we're crazy to be livin' out here on the river by ourselves. I think people that lives in cities must be **crazy**."

Culture and Heritage

When will we learn that we can't just allow the destruction of an entire cultural tradition without causing a significant amount of damage to the human soul in general and to our own individual spirit in particular? Where is our sense of vision, our perception of good? Are we just drifting like leaves on water, going this way and that with each small breath of breeze or flowing with each tiny current that nudges us one way or another? We need to do better.

We can't necessarily expect people in power to have vision, but we should be able to expect them to have the benefit of an accumulation of knowledge and wisdom. When can we expect that wisdom to begin coming into play? I had thought that I would begin this little book by listing the things that contribute, in an outstanding way, to the idea that the world we live in is essentially insane. And I may do it yet; I may provide examples of the things that I personally see as crazy, unreal, bizarre. But for now I'll ask you to go along with the thought, without requiring documentation. You know we live crazy lives, don't you? You have your own examples, your own list of things that make you wonder about your existence and about the sanity of the world we inhabit, things that wobble the mind, don't you? (see p. 88 "The Crazy Side of Life")

This is a book mostly about Cajuns, not the ones who have moved away to places like Houston, Atlanta, and Lafayette, away from the land, the big woods and the water, but the ones who have remained connected with those things--the "real Cajuns," I like to call them. These people and their culture are suffering an identity crisis of major proportions. I frequently find myself trying to describe to outsiders (Americans, as many Cajuns still call them) the essential difference between the average, standard-issue American mentality, and the true Cajun mentality.

As we say, "Time is money," and for most Americans (There are exceptions), if we're not making money, we're wasting time. Whether we admit it or not, whether we choose it and grasp it consciously or not, this is how we live. This determines our priorities, our actions and our system of values. For most Cajuns--true Cajuns, who revere their traditions and their identity--if we're not having fun, we're wasting our lives. The difference is clear and essential.

Henry David Thoreau would have made a good Cajun. He worshiped simplicity, and when he moved to a tiny cabin, constructed with his own hands and skills, he said: "I moved to the woods because I wished to live deliberately, to confront only the essential facts of life, and see if I could not learn what it had to teach, and not, when I came to die, discover that I had not lived."

Almost none (if not none) of the real Cajuns I write about and photograph own stocks, bonds, investments or portfolios, and I don't either. They don't feel really comfortable profiting from the efforts of others. If you ask them about the bottom line, they think you mean the catfish line that they placed close to the bottom of the bayou or river where they're fishing.

Dewey Patin with hoopnet under construction.

"Me I still make big nets. You can catch more fish in a net like that. I can almost stand up in a net like him.."

When real Cajuns construct a hoopnet, they know that they can buy the netting that others use to attach to their hoops, but they choose to make the netting themselves, hand-tying about 10,000 knots for each of the big nets.

I said, in *Atchafalaya Autumn*, that we, in South Louisiana, are living, more and more, in some sort of Cajun theme park. That which was genuine has become increasingly artificial. We have lost things that are not only valuable, but irreplaceable. (p.10)

The more that the Cajun culture is exploited for the goals and purposes of tourism alone, the less likely it is that anything valid and authentic about the culture will survive and endure.

Wrong Number Phone Call

Cajuns living in South Louisiana once spoke French—all of us did. That was before we were encouraged to believe that anyone who didn't speak standard English was doomed to second-class status. And if we failed to agree with that theory, we were reminded of it by punishments of various kinds administered by elementary school teachers and principals. We soon learned that it was to our advantage, in the short term, to drop the Cajun French and begin using standard English, at least on the school grounds. Eventually, Cajun French disappeared from our communities, except among the older people, especially those who had attended school before French was outlawed or who had hardly attended school at all. But most of us hung onto our accents when we spoke English, and even today, I consider it fortunate to encounter a child with a heavy Cajun accent.

"All right!" I say. "Cajun is still alive somewhere. We haven't been totally Americanized!"

About 15 years ago I was sitting in my house near Catahoula, Louisiana, and the phone rang. It was a wrong number call from a 3 or 4-year-old Cajun girl who thought she had dialed her father, apparently. She spoke with a heavy Cajun accent.

"Hello," I said.

There was a pause. "Umm. I could go pass the night at mah granmommy?"

"Aw, Ah don't tink so," I said, putting on a heavier accent to match hers. "How you gonna get way ova dere anyway?"

"Mah granmommy say she can come an' pick me up." she replied forcefully.

"What you mama got to say fuh dat?" I asked. Why was she call-
8

ing me, I wondered, unless her mother and the man the little girl thought she was talking to were separated, or the mother wanted me to tell the little girl no.

"Mah mama say hif it's O.K. wit' her, hif it's O.K. wit' you."

"Can you be good ova dere at granmommy?"

"For shore," she said "un-huh!"

"An you gonna tell granmommy hi for me?"

"Yeah," she said, extending the sound of the word, in expectation of my approval.

"O.K. Ah guess you can go, den."

"Oh, boy! T'anks! Bye." Click...dial tone.

Anna and Melissa Caffery with the shell of a 135 lb. snapping turtle

Oil tank converted to hunting camp on Bayou LaRompe

Sociology

I once read a sociological paper about poaching. It took the scholarly author a very long, complex paragraph to say this: Children of poachers are more likely to become poachers than other children are.

If I had that paragraph now, I would share it with you, but I don't, so I've attempted to write my own simple concept in that elevated, scholarly style. Please don't quit on me.

Whenever, in the course of human affairs, one culturally distinct group finds itself being absorbed into the ways and lifestyle of another, more numerous, more powerful group, there is bound to be trouble of an emotional, psychological nature, whether or not that trouble is recognized consciously by every member of the smaller group. Eventually the difficulty will become evident to almost all the members of that group, while most members of the larger group will hardly notice that anything of significance is happening. To the latter, if they ever think about it at all, the changes seem only natural, to be expected, even necessary, but of little consequence, unless the problem somehow spills over into their own lives.

If the group undergoing absorption and forced conformity accepts that situation without combativeness and confrontation, the process is smooth and seemingly insignificant. It seems that nothing of real value has been lost. Everything is all right.

But among the members of the smaller group are always certain individuals who are more sensitive to, and more aware of, the meaning of transition than those around them. These people usually suffer more and react more strongly than the others. If they struggle to maintain their unique traditions and their identity--the things that have made them who they are--they generally find themselves stifled, frustrated, controlled and manipulated from all sides, even from those of their own group. If these individuals are strong and determined, they may resist and even prevail for certain time while others of their group are being absorbed, like the victims of alien pods in the old movie "Invasion of the Body Snatchers." As each victim succumbed to sleep, too exhausted to resist any longer, he or she was taken over, body and soul, by the alien pod process. Eventually, all would apparently be lost. The transition would be complete and seamless.

The Cajun culture of South Louisiana finds itself in this unfortunate situation today. The struggle to maintain its traditions, its character and its very identity seems futile and bound to failure. Real Cajuns, those strong enough to insist on remaining Cajun, realize that their group is losing out to the prevailing society, and that society is essentially unbalanced and badly misdirected.

In other words, we Cajuns are being Americanized, and some of us don't like it at all. The Cajun Dream and the American Dream are not the same.

The pressure to Americanize, to standardize, to fold under, is too powerful to resist. **Look what happened to the Indians.**

What Does It Mean To Be Cajun?

My friend Roy Blanchard (*Cajun Families*, p 22) was asked once by Bill Geist of CBS News, "Roy, tell me, what is a Cajun?" Roy didn't bother to go into our ancestors leaving France in 1604, being deported from Eastern Canada in 1755, and finding their way, those who didn't get lost or die on the ships, to Louisiana to begin the struggle all over. Roy said, "A Cajun is a guy that's going to make it, no matter what." Doug Kershaw wrote a song with this line in it: "Gotta make a livin'; I'm a Louisiana man." He didn't mean get rich; he meant get by, subsist, endure, give life meaning by working hard, and by giving attention to the Cajun priorities--food, family, friends and fun (not to mention fishing, frogging, frying and Falstaff.....and fighting)

Real Cajuns today find themselves in the uncomfortable position of a person stepping from the land onto a boat that is beginning to move away. They have one foot on shore and one on the boat, and they can't decide whether it would be better to jump on the boat or jump back on land, and time is running out. If they don't decide and do something quickly, they risk falling into the water, whatever that means.

Crawfishing is part of our identity, like cooking and playing *bourrée* on houseboats. I read recently, in a book about the Tongass National Forest in Alaska, that many native Alaskan Indians there are,-- like French-speaking Cajuns here--subsistence fisherman and hunters. Not everyone in our society understands the significance of that traditional lifestyle.

Salmon fishing in Alaska

Some of the Native American people in Alaska have encountered problems similar to those faced by Cajuns, not only Cajuns trying to put food on the table but those trying to make a living in the swamps and bayous. The president of a sport-fishing association in Alaska commented on an indigenous tribe's challenge to a state subsistence law: "It's not like anybody really needs it [subsistence fishing]. We've got grocery stores, you know." (from *The Book of the Tongass* - 1999)

Chief Joseph

Thunder Rolling Down the Mountain (Chief Joseph) was born in 1840. He is recognized by many today, as well as during his lifetime, as one of the wisest, most honorable, fair-minded and peaceful individuals ever to walk on American soil.

He became Chief Joseph, of the Nez Percé tribe in 1871, in Oregon and Idaho. The U.S. government violated a treaty with the Nez Percé, and the tribe was relegated to a small reservation in Idaho, having had their previously-granted six million acres of land stolen and settled by white people. Battles followed between the Army and the Indians.

Eventually, Joesph and his people were captured and taken to Eastern Kansas, then to a reservation in Oklahoma Indian Territory. Chief Joseph, according to his doctor, died of a broken heart in

1904, by then back on another reservation in Northern Washington.

(Read a more detailed story of the life and struggles of Chief Joseph on the Internet.)

It seems sad and disrespectful to me when such an honorable person as Chief Joseph has his memory desecrated, primarily for commercial purposes, in the way these photos suggest. And can you imagine an Indian wanting to dam the Columbia River?

All photos: Bridgeport, WA

Speaking of Native Americans, here's what the late actor John Wayne had to say: "I don't feel we did wrong in taking this great country away from them. There were great numbers of PEOPLE who needed new land, and the Indians were selfishly trying to keep it for themselves."

It sounds like something the British might have said to justify stealing the Acadians' land and driving them out of Eastern Canada in 1755.

Food on the Road

Several years ago in June, Eursule Latiolais, from Catahoula, and her extended family (22 people total) decided to take a week-long trip to Gatlinburg in the Smokey Mountains. Rather than eat fast food along the road and in the eleven-bedroom house they had rented, they took all their food along with them–crawfish bisque, chicken

13

stew, venison /pork sausage, cooked white beans, boulettes, boudin, gumbo.....everything for three meals a day for a week, for 22 people. Real food is important to real Cajuns.

To the Latiolais family, fast food wasn't worth eating. I was telling that story to a friend one day and enjoying his amusement at the idea

of carrying a week's supply of real food along. "Wait a minute," he said. "Didn't you take a freezer full of sausage, boudin, crawfish stew and all to Virginia in a U-Haul trailer when you and your family moved up there?"

It is true. We had loaded a big chest-type freezer into a trailer and when we stopped in a motel, I had run an extension cord from the freezer into the room to keep our Cajun food frozen.

Cajuns and Pets

My wife of 27 years was only half Cajun, and she used to point out, quite correctly, that I seemed to have an aversion to making a living. That's not the only reason we're not married anymore, though we're good friends. I used to keep snakes, just a few of them and not that often either, in jars in the refrigerator (They're less active in the cold.) And then she came in from teaching one afternoon before I had time to get a couple of small alligators out of the sink (the zink, as some Cajuns still call it). Actually, she loved the pets, BUT...

As I came into the kitchen she was just landing about 8 feet from the zink, having recoiled in terror at being hissed and snapped at. (It may have been 10 feet--she danced ballet and was quite athletic). "You could have told me there were alligators in the sink," she commented. "I didn't know you were home yet," I pleaded. "Is there anything else I should watch out for?" she asked. "There's a baby owl in the living room," I said, "but he doesn't bite." Pause: "Oh, and there's a hawk on the breezeway. Sorry."

Greg and red shouldered hawk

Baby owl and kitten friend

While I'm on the subject of Cajuns and pets, let me point out something about dogs and cats, mostly dogs: Whatever psychological aberration requires some people to allow dogs to live with them in their houses and even sleep in their beds, most real Cajuns are not afflicted with it. It disturbs me, on a certain level, to see dogs and cats mistreating people so cruelly, controlling their lives--you know what I mean. You've seen it, haven't you? Cajuns love their dogs, but we live in a relatively mild climate--dogs can survive well outside. They have more fun and autonomy there anyway. I have a nephew and niece with two wiener dogs who bark so loudly, even at people they've seen a hundred times, that everyone has to wait a minute or two before speaking, after entering their house, so that the dogs can get through their noise period. One is on Prozac. No kidding!

I have other horror stories about people with dogs in their houses, but I'll limit myself to only one more (I know that some of my readers are afflicted with the deficiency mentioned earlier). I was at the home of friends near New Iberia once, with several other people. It was an informal gathering mostly to visit and eat boneless chicken stuffed with crawfish etouffée dressing. The hosts were not Cajun, but they could bake a stuffed chicken anyway. But that's not the point. The point is that they, too, had a couple of loud dogs in the house. I can't tell you the name of the breed. They were stumpy and short-haired like bulldogs, but with almost no snout at all. (You people with the affliction could name them, huh?) Anyway, one of the guests bent over to pick something off the floor and her prescription sunglasses fell out of her shirt pocket. As quick as a great blue heron spearing a minnow, one of those ugly dogs has pounced on the glasses and crushed them in its jaws--glass, plastic, metal and all. They were ruined (the glasses, not the dogs. The dogs bad been ruined long before the night began).

They were properly scolded in baby-talk English. To the dogs it sounded like "Blah! Blah! Blah!". To us humans, it sounded like, "Now Billy and Princess, you know that's not how you should act around guests. You tell the nice lady how sorry you are, etc, etc." I would have made sure they were sorry. I would have exiled them to the great outdoors for the rest of their short-legged lives.

~

And then there was Myrtle. Myrtle and Harold Bigler lived on the main channel of the Atchafalaya just about all their lives (pp 48 *Atchafalaya Autumn* and 73 *Cajun Families*). They were Cajun by mentality and lifestyle, though not by heritage. They had no children, but they averaged six dogs in the house. Actually, the dogs could leave the house whenever they wanted, but they seldom did. (This is not horror story #3, which I promised to spare you. This is a story of love and devotion, in one way or another.)

I had gone to Myrtle's place one day (Harold had died a couple of years earlier, and though Myrtle was 92, she lived out there alone, 13 miles by boat from other human beings). My ex-wife, Bubbles, accompanied me, as did a couple from Colorado who didn't know me very well and had never met Myrtle.

When we walked into her house, there were several dogs there, but one of them didn't get up to greet us. He seemed weak and sick, and, in fact, he died while we were there visiting, so Myrtle was not in a good mood.

"They been poisonin' for roaches out here, Craig, and they killed my dog, them sheriff deputies," she said.

"How old was your dog, Myrtle?" I should never had asked.

"Well, he was 16 or so, but it's the roach poison what kilt him, Craig!"

"Did it kill any of the younger dogs, Myrtle?" I was pushing it.

"Naw, the others is all right, but it sure got Snow. They killed Boxer, too, fed him chicken bones."

I pointed out that I fed my dogs chicken bones all the time and none of them had developed any problems. And I reminded Myrtle that Boxer had gotten into the boat of some visitors from Baton Rouge once and eaten a huge box of fried chicken, bones and all. He even ate the greasy box. (*Cajun Families*, p. 80).

"Well, it don't kill 'em every time, Craig. It kills 'em when it gets caught in their throat and chokes 'em."

Then Myrtle chose to take it out on me to relieve her bad mood:

"Craig," she said (She knew my name was Greg, but she was hard headed), "the last time you and your friend Tom was out here, y'all ate the whole chicken I had baked, y'all was so hung over."

"Myrtle," I said, "you told us you had baked that chicken for us, and it wasn't very big anyway, and I don't drink, so I don't get hung over. I can't speak for Tom. You ask Bubbles if I ever get hung over. We were married for 27 years; she should know."

"Naw, Craig; Bubbles gonna take up for you," she said.

"No she won't, Myrtle; we've been divorced for years."

"That don't matter, Craig; she's gonna take up for you anyway."

Myrtle went on being nice to the others for a few minutes. Then she turned to me again: "Craig--and I'll tell you somethin' else--you dye your hair!"

"What? I don't dye my hair!" I pleaded.

"You sure do, Craig. Your beard's gray and you hair's dark."

"Myrtle, you ask Bubbles if I dye my hair."

"Naw, Craig; Bubbles gonna take up for you," she said.

"No, she won't, Myrtle; we've been divorced for years. She won't take up for me. She'll tell you the truth."

Well, it went on like that for a while longer until I had enough. By that time the couple from Colorado figured me for an alcoholic who dyed his hair.

"Myrtle," I said. "You've been so ugly to me today, I'm not go-ing to help bury your dog." (It's easy to bury a dog out on the river because the soil is all sediment. It's sandy and digs easily.) I went out and split firewood to ease my frustration, while Bubbles and the Colorado couple buried the dog. Then we left, but that's not the end of the story. Every time after that (for 3 years) when I visited Myrtle she would say to me, "Craig, them folks from Colorado you done brought out was the finest people I ever met--They buried my dog!"

For 35 years I split Myrtle and Harold's firewood, patched their fences and their roof, carried their groceries to them and their social security checks, took them to the doctor for check-ups and treatment, picked up and delivered their medicine, but I refused to bury Old Snow, and she never let me forget it.

Myrtle and the Colorado couple

Of course, Myrtle had a right to be upset. Her dogs were like children to her, and one of them had died (of roach poisoning).

The Spirit of Myrtle Bigler

In 1995, the day after Myrtle died, I called the actress Barbara Hershey in California; Barbara had modeled herself after Myrtle for her role in the movie "Shy People," and she had become very close to Harold and Myrtle. As soon as she answered and I identified myself, she said, "You don't have to tell me why you called. Myrtle died yesterday around midday, didn't she?"

Harold and Myrtle at home with Barbara Hershey, 1986

In August 2002 I received a phone call from a woman who was looking for a copy of my first book, *Seasons of Light in the Atchafalaya Basin*, which has been out-of-print for many years. Gwen Lile was the wife of a great nephew of Myrtle's, Robert.

Gwen told me the following story over the phone. It gave me the *frissons*, and I told her that if she wrote the story to me in a letter, I would give her a copy of *Seasons*. Below is her letter. I have no reason to think that any of it is fabricated.

August 2002

Dear Greg,

Late September of last year we had gone to the camp. (The camp is about a hundred yards from Harold and Myrtle's old house on the Atchafalaya.) Robert had been up for 24 hours. We left when he got off work that morning. I couldn't wait to get a good night's sleep. I took some Tylenol PM to make sure I slept good. Everybody had their own bunk. The boys were on the top ones. Around 1 AM Landen (11 years old) woke me up. I got up, looked in the kitchen and saw a fire. I woke Robert up, and Landen got Justin (age 6) out of the other top bunk and brought us outside. Justin and me stayed on the front porch. Landen went back to help Robert put out the fire. After everything was over I sat crying in the bed, trying to remember the "Our Father." I made the boys stay with me for a while. Then Landen wanted to sleep in his top bunk, so he climbed the ladder, laid down and told me, "Don't worry, Mom; I'll be O.K." Robert was in his bunk, under Landen's. Finally Justin and me fell asleep.

In the morning I was thanking God and Landen for saving our lives. Robert and Justin were still sleeping. I asked Landen what had happened to wake him up, because I hadn't smelled any smoke, but it was so thick when we got up you couldn't see anything. He said he heard Aunt Myrtle singing to him like she always does, but this time he saw a bright blue light in the kitchen, just like the one he sees at Aunt Myrtle's house. But it was much brighter so he got up to look and see what it was; that's when he saw the fire and woke me up. I told him how proud I was of him.

He said, "You know, Mom, you didn't have to come check on me last night. I told you I was O.K." I told him, "I didn't get up to check on you. Justin was sleeping with me after the fire and I didn't want to wake him up. Landen said, "Mama, I saw you climb on the. ladder and look straight at me and smile," I told him that must have been his angel checking on him and then he said, "You know what, Mama: it wasn't you; it was Aunt Myrtle."

About an hour later Justin and Robert woke up. I asked Justin if he remembered anything about last night. He had no clue. He had slept through the whole thing. The only thing he said was, "Mama, who was that lady that kept singing?" (Justin never knew Myrtle; she died seven years ago.) I asked him what she was signing and he hummed the tune for me. He said she sang real pretty. Landen's eyes got real big; he told me later it was the same song he had heard. Needless to say, we believe in our hearts that Aunt Myrtle saved our lives. I hope this makes sense.

Take care and God Bless,   Gwen Lile

The Bigler home on the river

The camp nearby

Divorce in Catahoula

When I was growing up near Catahoula, in St. Martin Parish, divorce was almost unknown. There was an occasional quiet separation, but, except for two Buddhists, the community was all Catholic, and divorce was late getting there.

Finally, one particular middle-aged couple decided to end their marriage, and I wish now that I had been a photographer then, to record the effects. The woman hired a carpenter to saw their house

in two. She moved her half, consisting of the front porch, the living room and the front bedroom to Henderson, 10 miles away. She left her husband with the back bedroom and the kitchen, as well as the inside wall that had separated what became the two halves of their little house. That wall had mirrors and photographs hanging on it, wall paper covering it, no windows, etc. It looked like an inside wall, since that's what it was, but it became the outside wall of his house.

Either he was crushed by her departure or he just didn't care. He left the pictures and mirrors and wall paper as they had always been. He just built a set of steps to enter his half house through the doorway to the kitchen. I wish I could have photographed the place-- It stayed that way for a long time, until rain and sun had faded the pictures and demolished the wall paper, but he went on living there as though nothing had happened, and everybody got used to the sight. I just didn't realize then that I was a photographer.

~

On another occasion involving Cajuns, though I had become a photographer, I wasn't there to take the potential prize-winning picture. It was a Saturday afternoon when a friend of mine was doing some clean-up work at a construction site, with the assistance of an employee of his. The workman stepped on an exposed nail, which went all the way through his foot, so my friend called several doctors until he found one who was willing to help out on a Saturday afternoon. "I've got to go to the clinic anyway," the doctor said. "Some guy got bit by a turtle. Meet me there about 3 P.M." My friend and his employee found, when they reached the clinic, two other men waiting for the doctor. One had an alligator snapping turtle attached to his nose. It's not something you see every day, so my friend asked

Blake Blanchard and snapping turtle head

how it happened. "Well, I raise snapping turtles, in cages about 3 feet off the ground, and Placide there decides to open the door and get a better look. The turtle you see there was right behind the door and when Placide stuck his ugly face in there, it got him on the nose. And you know how it is with those damn turtles; they ain't gonna let go."

The man with the turtle was holding it up with one hand on its underside, so that the turtle's weight wouldn't tear his nose off, and he was in pain. The doctor was late. Finally, the man with the turtle said to his buddy, "Look, I got to have a cigarette." Imagine the photograph--a man sitting there, cross-legged, holding up a turtle hanging off his nose with one hand, holding him a little to the side, so that he could smoke a cigarette. I missed it.

Finally the doctor came in and cut the turtle's head off and pried the jaws open. It will probably never happen again, but if it does, and it happens to you, all you have to do it stick a piece of wire up the turtle's nose and tickle it. Placide, him, he didn't know that. He was one of those Cajuns who have lost their connection to the big woods and the swamp. He had moved to Lafayette.

Cooking and Whatnot

My closest neighbor (a mile away) for many years is a man named Errol Verret, and he hasn't lost his connection with the Cajun ways. Many real Cajuns are very self-sufficient, with skills and talents that most people have lost, but Errol is an extreme case. He built his own house, for example, and his own boat. He's a fisherman and hunter;

he operates a small sawmill; he's a welder and carpenter. He's a musician and song-writer who played accordion for years with the Beau Soleil Cajun Band. He makes and sells accordions. He's a state forester. And he cooks like a chef. One day I was telling Errol about an article I had read, in an outdoor magazine, concerning the European ring-necked dove, a species that had been introduced unintentionally into Florida and was spreading across the South, into Louisiana and Texas. Some environmentalists were concerned that these doves might take over habitat on which native species of birds depend.. It seemed to be a big problem. Errol's response consisted of only one

Tony Latiolais and Errol Verret take a break from boat building

question, the question a true Cajun would naturally ask: "Well," he said, "how does it cook up?"

It's a well known fact that Cajuns are great cooks and that we eat just about anything that crawls, swims or flies or walks on four legs.

It's said that one essential characteristic distinguishes a Cajun zoo from a standard American zoo. While the American zoo has an information plaque identifying the species by scientific name and common name, habitat, food source, etc., the Cajun zoo's plaque lists only the common name, plus one or two good recipes.

And it's not true that all real Cajuns are poachers. I myself know

3 or 4 who would never do that kind of thing, or so they tell me. You've heard the story of the Cajun on trial for poaching who claimed that night heron (gros-bec) tasted like bald eagle. Whoever told the story got it backward: A real Cajun can make even a tough old bald eagle taste like gros bec-- whatever that tastes like--(Don't ask me-- my dad was a game warden.)

Most Cajun men who weren't on the front lines in France translating between American and French forces, were behind the lines cooking, during the 1st and 2nd World Wars. Real Cajun men, young and old, are as much at ease in the kitchen as they are in a duck blind or raising crawfish traps in the swamp. People who really like to eat good food learn to cook. With Cajuns, it comes with the territory and the lifestyle. It's understood and expected, without regard to age or sex.

~

From the first night in October when the temperature drops into the 50's, to the last cool night in April, I'm cooking on my woodstove. It was April 9, 2003.

You may wonder what a self-employed Cajun might be doing on an afternoon like this. It's cold for this time of year (48 degrees F. at 2PM). I would be setting out the forty-two new crawfish traps I picked up in Catahoula today from Oline Guidry (see *Cajun Families*, page30). But the water in the Basin has dropped really fast when it should have been rising, and I can't get into the part of the swamp where I had planned to put my traps until it goes up a foot or two.

So I lit my woodstove late this morning, using cypress for kindling and live oak for cooking, and now I have three iron pots going--one with ducks (two mallards, one teal, one wood duck), one with squirrel sauce picante, and the big one with chicken and pork sausage gumbo. I don't hunt at all: My cousin Pat and my son Emile give me ducks, and Roy Blanchard gives me squirrels and venison/pork sausage. There were homemade biscuits in the oven.

It can be dangerous to cook on a woodstove. It causes gross over-eating-- The last time I cooked chicken and sausage gumbo there, I ate about half the pot of gumbo and all of a batch of biscuits I had put into the oven just at the right moment. Ask any Cajun who uses a wood cookstove--the food is better. Or maybe it's the connection to an earlier, simpler, more focused time. In any case, you could hurt yourself cooking on a woodstove. Also, you can put your mug of fresh coffee at the right place on the stove surface to keep it just warm enough for drinking while you're cooking and tasting. On the surface of my cast-iron woodstove are these small, raised letters: "HOT when in use." (No kidding, huh?) I tried to dry my pants and socks on a woodstove while camping out on the river one winter night. It was something of a disaster.

Sophie Guirard, age 7, crawfishing in a pond near Catahoula, Louisiana

Lake Bruin Heron
for Greg Guirard

by Sidney Creaghan

One lone Great Blue Heron
waits like a king
on the railing
of the ramshackle old pier.
He stands as still as any spire.
Like Mahatma Gandhi
his legs are sinew and ligament
like Gandhi
he knows exactly what to do,
like Gandhi he knows how
to hold still.
The Great Blue Heron cocks his
black wild eye toward me as I sit
with my pencil moving across the
image of his contour appearing
like a miracle on my page.
Then without visible preparation
he lifts, a master of air,
spreads without fanfare
silent across
the lake.
I sit in reverance.
I know to hold still.

Carol Patin, Fred Laviolette and
Dewey Patin, St. Martin Parish

Carol, Fred and Dewey with
world record blue catfish,
128 lbs., August, 1986

Real Cajuns don't use the word "very." Instead of that adverb, they double or triple the adjective. I asked a fisherman what kind of turtle he was eating one night. "I'm not sure," he said, "but the back was bumpy, bumpy bumpy."

Richard Olivier, Lake Dauterive

C. J. Dupré, Pierre Part

Blanc Courville, Catahoula

Alcide Verret, Bayou
Sorrel

**Our salvation as Cajuns lies in our recognizing the validity
of our cultural identity and insisting on its protection and
continuation.**

Genevieve Arnaud, Lake
Dauterive

Ernest Melancon,
Catahoula

Connie and
Verlie Serrette,
Henderson

Connie Serrette and
grandson with hoopnet

Connie Serrette's grandson has fun watching Connie put together an 18-foot-long hoopnet, but he will never be a commercial fisherman in the Atchafalaya like his grandfather. That life is ending, unfortunately.

Bernard Blanchard, Catahoula

Cypress Gargoyle,
Cocodrie Swamp

Hospitality

The genuine hospitality of Cajuns is legendary and well established, but a couple of instances in which I was personally involved, bear telling about here.

I received a phone call, a few years ago, from a man I knew in Lafayette. He wanted to know if I could arrange a swamp tour, in small boats, for about 25 wedding guests. I called several crawfishing friends (It was the off season, in the fall) and five of them agreed to conduct the 2-3 hour tour on a Saturday. Eventually, some of the guests needed to use a toilet, and there aren't any public restrooms out in the swamps, so the boat drivers decided to stop at the houseboat of a friend , Tee Clet Lasseigne, and ask permission to use his.

Tee Clet Lasseigne's houseboat at Bayou Cocodrie, near Catahoula

He welcomed everybody aboard his large houseboat, where he and some of his friends were spending the weekend and beginning to fry catfish and sac-a-lait that they had caught that morning. Not only did he let the wedding guests use his toilet. He insisted that they eat with him and his friends, who had caught more fish than they could eat by themselves. They readily agreed, and all 25 guests and 5 boat driver guides were fed--at no charge, of course. The true Cajun houseboat owner figured that these strangers had done him a favor-- He didn't have to deal with the problem of what to do with all those extra fish.

~

I worked on a television commercial in the little Cajun town of Cutoff, LA, on Bayou Lafourche, for a few days in the early 90s. We filmed a Cajun crab, crawfish and shrimp boil, with music and dancing and a shrimp and oyster boat parade, next to a gas station owned by a man named Philip Guidry. Philip was incredibly generous and helpful over the two-day period we worked there. I didn't know that he had even learned my name because our crew was large and he was meeting and dealing with all of us while keeping his gas station in operation.

Dudley Bernard telling stories to an
oyster-shucking friend on Bayou Lafourche

About six months later, I was driving to Grand Isle, on the Gulf, to spend a few days with a friend; and we stopped at Philip Guidry's place. I would have not remembered his name, but it was right there on the building--Philip Guidry Exxon. He walked out, all smiles and welcoming handshakes, saying, "Hey, Greg, my old friend. How you been?" We talked -- well, like old friends.

We gassed up and were ready to leave when Philip said, "Where y'all gonna eat dinner?" It was noon.

"I don't know," I said. We'll get a hamburger down the road. "Oh, no," he said. "Y'all don't do that! My wife cooked a big meal and I'm going home to eat. Y'all come with me." So we followed him to his home across the bayou, and while we were stuffing ourselves with his wife's baked chicken, friend catfish, rice dressing, etc., Philip said, "Where y'all plannin' to stay down in Grand Isle?"

"I don't know. We'll find a cabin to rent or something," I said.

"Oh, no!" Philip said. "We got a nice camp down there, right on the water. I'll give you the key. Stay as long as y'all want."

As we got up to leave, with his camp key in my pocket, Philip said, as if he had forgotten something he should have remembered, "Wait a minute... what y'all gonna eat down there in Grand Isle?"

"I don't know," I said. "We'll buy some shrimp or some crabs or something when we get there."

"Oh, no!" Philip said for the third time in two hours. "We got a freezer full of fish and shrimp and stuff. Get your ice chest."

So he filled my ice chest, and we were off to Grand Isle. When we got back to Cutoff a few days later to drop off his key, Philip came out, all smiles again; "Pick up the key next time y'all come through," he said, "And if y'all have time, come and eat with us," as if I would be doing him a favor.

When I tried to explain to Philip Guidry what that kind of hospitality means in a world like the one we live in today, he played it down, as if it had been of no consequence at all.

"Aw, we fish a lot. We had more than we could ever eat. And as for the camp, nobody was using it. You might as well use it, hein?"

That's what it means to be a real Cajun.

Ça C'est Lafayette

Many people, seeing the postcard photos below, have asked me why the one of my son Jean-Paul is labeled "The Lafayette Approach." Well, it's hard to be tactful about something like this, so I'll just describe what I have observed and what others have observed as well: Lafayette people just don't know how to act out in the Basin, for the most part. There are exceptions, of course. But mostly, Lafayette-dwellers are out of their element. They wear street shoes. They're clumsy in boats. They try to eat live alligators head-first, etc.

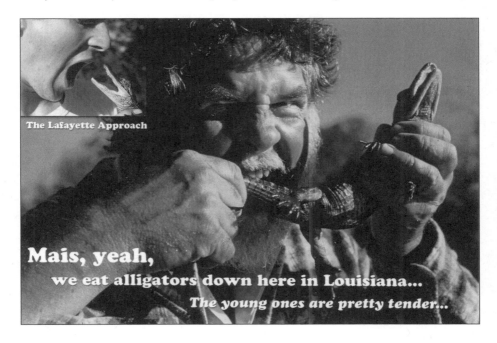

The Lafayette Approach

Mais, yeah, we eat alligators down here in Louisiana... *The young ones are pretty tender...*

Let me give you a couple more examples: Years ago my ex-wife and I got peppered with bird shot from a hunter on the bank who could see us coming a half mile away. Luckily it was cold and we were wearing heavy coats. He was shooting at a woodcock, he said. Guess where he was from. Right! Lafayette.

On another occasion I was about to drive my truck and trailer out of a parking place near the boat ramp at Bayou Benoit. Another driver backed up right in front of me, blocking my way. His intention was to back his boat trailer into the water and launch the boat.

But first he needed to unload stuff from his car into his boat—lots of stuff. I got out of my truck and waited. He smiled at me a couple of times, but made no effort to hurry or move out of the way. I timed him—14 minutes. Finally he launched the boat and pulled his trailer out to go and park. When he returned, I walked up and asked him, "Are you from Lafayette by any chance?" He was all surprised: "How'd you know that?" he asked. "Just a lucky guess," I said.

I'm not the only one who's noticed this condition. In fact, there's a long-standing expression to describe it: "Ça c'est Lafayette," meaning "That's Lafayette for you."

Don't be calling me to complain about this observation, OK? I already admitted that there are a few exceptions. Maybe you're one of them. **Maybe....**

Nicknames

Almost all Cajun boys have nicknames that stay with them all their lives. My nickname was "Dancing Bear." My high school mates had nicknames like "Squeeky," "Gumsy," "Spike," "Serpent," "Chaoui," "Pas Nouri," "Shovlin' Education," "Cyclops," "Sarrab," "Canaille."

I have an old Breaux Bridge telephone directory here, with names like Rebellion "Boo Boo" Durio and Philip "T-Sue" Roberts. Other nicknames in the same directory include Big Man, Shorty, Pee Wee, Boonie, Jap, Shine, Malot, Corn Cob, Pipsey, T-Boy, Boggay, Back-Track, Blue, Black, Yogi, Tree, T-Colo, Two Bit, Tickey, and Jaybird.

At that time there were three Terry LeBlancs in the Breaux Bridge area. They are differentiated in the directory by their nicknames: "Boogie," "Snoopy," and "Squirt."

Raymond Melancon, from Catahoula, has done a lot of aluminum welding for me. One day I was speaking to another Melancon who just couldn't place Raymond, though they lived only a quarter mile apart. Finally, I said, "Hell, Russell, he lives right there (I pointed). In fact, he's your uncle!"

"Oh!" Russell said, "You mean Mookey! That's right, his name is Raymond." I had never called him Mookey, and Russell had never called him Raymond.

I attended a court case involving the crawfishermen vs. the big landowners in the Atchafalaya Basin yesterday (September 14, 2006) and was a little surprised to hear the judge call the opposing lawyers by their first names as well as their nicknames. The attorneys called each other by their nicknames and first names as well. They called the judge not "your honor" but "judge." I should not have been surprised. This is Cajun Country.

Squirrel Quesadillas and Caregivers

There I was, sitting on the sofa last night, enjoying my squirrel quesadillas, not bothering even one of the other 6 billion screwed-up humans running around on the face of this insane planet and —wham—the phone rings. Don't get me wrong, whatever else you do; I am one of those poor souls who, in order to compensate for some deficiency in his childhood, will do almost anything for almost anybody, operating under the wild delusion that doing so will some-how correct the dysfunction of my earlier years, though I admit that sometimes I do it subconsciously. And thank God for that, huh? If I did that kind of thing consciously, on a regular basis, you could just about throw me in the nuthouse, but I can't blame myself for the things I do subconsciously. And you can't blame me for the original deficiency either, even though I've probably passed it on to my own kids by now, not knowing what I was doing, as they say.

Anyway, I was set up just right on the sofa. There was a good movie coming on TV. I had my squirrel quesadillas all hot and runny with cheese and barbecue sauce to cover the fact that the squirrel was a little freezer-burned. I don't hunt squirrel myself, of course — those cute little things. I used to, don't get me wrong. I would just as soon shoot a squirrel or a duck or a deer as send a donation to the Audubon Society, but that was when my grandfather was living. The squirrels I eat now and the ducks too, if you don't mind my saying so, are almost always a little freezer-burned, because they're given to me by my friend, Roy, who hunts all the time. He won't be giving me stuff from his freezer until his success in the current hunting season guarantees him that he won't need all the stuff he killed and froze last year and didn't get around to eating. Then he unloads on me, to clean his freezer out and make room for this year's kill. I never get any of the fresh stuff, under this system. Don't get me wrong: freezer-burned squirrel is better than no squirrel, and Roy is a generous man.

Roy Blanchard

You're wondering what my inability to procure fresh game has to do with the death of my grandfather, or you should be, if you're paying attention. Well, that's a long story. It begins somewhere around the middle of the last century, when I began hunting with my grandfather. Or were you wondering who was calling? We'll get to that later.

My grandfather was a fine man, and everybody knows it, even those who never met him. He treated everybody equally. He never yelled at us for being kids, even when my brother and I were gutting rabbits at the kitchen sink, really stinking up the place and making yuck sounds while he was trying to do paper work on the dining table in the same room — we lived in a camp. I don't know if you ever cleaned rabbits inside, but the smell could end your rabbit-eating days right there, if you're sensitive to that kind of thing. It was too cold and drizzly outside, which is why we were doing it in the kitchen sink. Every time I yelled at my own kids many years

Wade O. Martin, Sr.

later I would think about my grandfather and how he never yelled at me or my brother or our crazy cousins. How could he do it? I always wondered. Don't get me wrong: We got yelled at plenty. My mother took care of that, but that's another story. At least, I think it is. I'm not sure. It's not that easy to say where one story ends and another one begins, you know? Anyway, my grandfather, who died when I was 19, was pretty much the moderating influence in the dysfunctional nature of my upbringing.

If you were paying attention, you're wondering what all that has to do with my giving up on hunting. And don't worry about the phone call. That's not the point right now.

To hunt with my grandfather was like no other experience in life for me. He had a way of making a kid feel important, like you counted for something, you know? In spite of his many obligations and responsibilities as an elected public official, he used to take us with him for two weeks every December and we'd all go hunting along with a group of his sawmill workers. We lived on a boat at first, with a Model-A Ford engine and bunk beds and later in a slapped-together camp on top of an Indian mound out in the Atchafalaya Basin. It was so cold in that camp I sometimes slept almost under the big wood stove and kept feeding it all night to keep myself and the others from freezing. (Read William Faulkner's *The Bear*)

Wherever we were hunting in the Basin on Saturday afternoon, we always had to make our way to the Catahoula landing by early Sunday morning, because attending Catholic mass was required, no excuses. We would dock there and my mother would pick us up and drive us about a mile to St. Rita's, dirty and wearing our hunting clothes. We would never go the two miles to our house because my grandfather had so much work waiting for him there and so many people trying to get him on the phone that we would never have made it back into the Basin for a second week of hunting if we had tried to go home even for a few minutes.

It always embarrassed me to see my grandfather in his muddy hunting jacket in church, his sheriff's revolver in a holster on his belt. Ever since he had been sheriff (five terms) many years earlier, he always wore that .38 special while hunting, and in his mind we were still on the hunt, the church service being only a brief interrup-

tion. (My grandfather was Wade O. Martin, Sr., and his mother was Ida Guilbeau. One of his many brothers dressed for the first time in a tuxedo to attend a big wedding. He liked the way he looked and felt in formal dress so much that he wore a tux every day for the rest of his life. Another of his brothers, just a boy, walked all the way from Grand Coteau, where he was in school, to Arnaudville during the flu epidemic of 1918, so that he could die at home.)

We almost all died on one of our two-week hunting trips in the early 1950s. It was a bitterly cold day, and we were moving from one part of the Basin to another in an old cabin boat powered by the Model-A gasoline engine. We had eaten a big meal at noon (*grosbec* and *bec-croche sauce picante*), so everyone but my grandfather and Junice Savoy lay down to take a nap and stay warm. There were bunks on both sides of the boat and across the stern. My grandfather was driving the boat, with a small opening in the window to his left, for ventilation, and talking to Junice. Everyone else was sleeping.

Junice Savoy and his wife Sophie on "Southern Comfort" set

For some reason that we will never know, my brother Jim, after a half hour or so, rolled off his bunk and fell on the floor, but he didn't wake up. My grandfather steered the boat toward the river bank and asked Junice to go out and tie up. As soon as Junice stood up he fell to his knees. The old engine had an exhaust leak, and the cabin had filled with carbon monoxide. We were mostly unconscious by that time and only minutes from death.

If my brother had not rolled off onto the floor, we would all have died that cold day, with the possible exception of my grandfather, and you wouldn't be reading this book.

~

For a week before the big hunt – of course, we kids hunted rabbits and squirrels on the side, as they say, all winter, but this was the BIG hunt – we would dedicate ourselves to getting ready. We would sit with my grandfather every evening and listen to him telling stories about the old days, about the hunting dogs he had raised, about deer hunts and bear hunts on the Alabama River (in South Central Louisiana; go figure), all the while polishing his leather boots or sharpening his knives and making sure all his equipment was in good shape and ready. Dismantling and oiling his guns was the final part of this traditional ceremony. All this went on right in the living room, and my mother knew better than to try to interfere. My grandfather was one person she couldn't control, and she didn't even try.

If the phone rang (Our entire number was 52), it was almost always for my grandfather. Someone needed electricity or a telephone; there was a problem with flood control or transportation, or whatever, that needed his attention. (He was Public Service Commissioner). We would sit and wait and fiddle around with something or other until he got back into the circle and the stories continued. That's what it was, I think--the stories. Even in the hunting camp itself, whether we were having successful hunts or not, the stories were the big thing. Some event from the day's hunt would remind him of the past, and while the onions and venison sizzled and then boiled and rice steamed on the woodstove, we would be treated to another tale, full of brave dogs and courageous men and miles and miles of untouched wilderness full of bears and deer and bobcats and panthers and alligators as long as a 3-man pirogue (That's about 14 feet). Not long after my grandfather died, I quit hunting.

In a way, my mother was glad to get rid of us when we went on the big hunt. It gave her time to clean the smell of gun oil and leather saddle soap out of the living room. At least she directed the cleaning. She directed the cooking too and somehow she became known as a great cook. It makes you wonder, if you know what I mean, about the truth in any concept or situation you hear about. If you know what's really going on, it's all different from what everybody else thinks. The only thing my mother actually cooked herself was something she called marzetti. It's a mixture of noodles and ground meat and onions and corn and tomatoes, baked in a casserole dish with cheese. It was the only thing she ever served to company. If there was company coming, we knew what we'd be eating – marzetti. My mother never taught me to cook – I learned in the hunting camp. Junice Savoy taught me. When Junice died, he lay in his casket wearing a camouflage hunting jacket and hunting cap. Junice was a good man. Dewey Patin hunted with us, too.

If you want to read a good collection of stories, one of which concerns a mother who cooks a terrible-tasting marzetti-like dish every time there's company, read Lewis Nordan's *Welcome to the Arrow-Catcher Fair*.

Myrtle Bigler and Bridget Guirard - 1993

Dewey Patin and friend--2002

40

Becoming Cajun
by Sheryl St.Germain

My father's mother, Celeste Fontenot, was Cajun. My father was not proud of his Cajun blood, however, and never taught us French, although it was the first language he learned. Many from his generation were made to feel ashamed of their ethnic roots, so much so that the language and culture almost died out in the middle of the twentieth century. In addition to being Cajun, Celeste Fontenot was also deaf and mute. The fact that his mother was both Cajun and a deaf-mute was a double blow to my father's pride—and he didn't bother teaching us much sign language either.

Celeste was born and lived much of her life in Ville Platte, a small town in French Louisiana. She moved to New Orleans when she married my grandfather, and though she would return to visit Ville Platte frequently, my father never took us to visit the relatives there. A shatteringly thorough silence about that side of the family prevented any of the children from getting to know our rural relatives or much about their culture. I felt this silence even more keenly after I moved to the Cajun mecca of Lafayette, about two hours west of New Orleans, to take my first teaching job. There I began to be exposed, on a daily basis, to students and colleagues who were full-blooded Cajuns and had lived in French Louisiana all their lives. The local NPR station played almost as much Cajun music, it seemed to me, as classical music. Cajun restaurants were on every corner; Cajun music and food festivals took place every spring. Even some television programming was in French.

I remember clearly lying in bed one night in Lafayette listening to a Cajun music program, struggling to understand this particular brand of French, and wondering how anyone could really like this music with its wailing, whining singing and shrill, insistent fiddling. This culture I didn't understand was, by blood, my own, and I didn't have a clue about what that meant.

I would come, in the years I spent in Lafayette, to love the music and the culture. I would find that these people—my people—possessed joyous, raucous spirits. Lovers of drink and dance, wonderful cooks and outdoorsmen and women, whenever they spoke, whether in English or in French, their speech was buoyant and musical. I bought a house in Lafayette, near the university, a house made of cypress, that wood so impervious to rot. I planted cypress trees and river birch in the backyard, an oak in the front. I learned Cajun French, and published a translation of a book-length poem about the Cajun diaspora.

Four years later, disappointed with the disparaging attitude toward education in Louisiana and a university system that didn't give even cost-of- living raises to faculty for three years running, I left to take a better paying job at a private liberal arts college in Illinois. When I visited Lafayette last year I drove by that house where I'd come home to my Cajun ancestry. The river birch towers over the back of it, its cinnamon bark cracking and peeling in beautifully intimate patterns, as I knew it would. The cypress and oak are almost as tall as the apex of the roof of the house, and the oak has spread its branches over one half of the front yard. I reached my arms around the river birch's shaggy trunk, breathed in the birch-air, celebrated and mourned the roots it had grown that I had not.

A few years after her husband Albin's death Celeste became ill with a heart condition. She spent her last hours in a hospital. There, the nurses and doctors caring for her did not speak sign language. They tied her arms down to prevent her pulling out her IV, which effectively took away her voice. When my mother visited her, Celeste signed over and over, hands tied down, the letter "A"—a fist with the thumb pointed up, the sign for Albin. She died with both hands clenched, thumbs up, her body, in its last moments, forming the name of her husband.

It's frightening how fate can sometimes converge, or conspire with dreams, fears, or desires to push you in a direction you might never have gone. Last year, around the time I was thinking about my grandmother and about my Cajun heritage, I became suddenly and permanently deaf in one ear, victim of something doctors call sud-den sensory-neural hearing loss, a poorly understood phenomenon that is, evidently, not all that uncommon. My condition is not related to my grandparents' since theirs was congenital, but I had a lot of time to think, as I struggled with a considerable diminishment of hearing, about this new, unwanted connection I now had with them. I began to sense that the silence my father had passed along to me about them could easily become a more literal one. If I had lost the hearing in one ear, why not eventually the other? I needed to open my ears, and my heart, to everything that was around me while there was still time.

You see why it's called **Bayou** Mercier Road? Sometimes, after a big rain, it is more bayou than road. It leads to my house.

Cajun
by Sheryl St. Germain

I want to take the word back into my body, back
from the northern restaurants with their neon signs
announcing it like a whore. I want it to be private again,
I want to sink back into the swamps that are nothing
like these clean restaurants, the swamps
with their mud and jaws and eyes that float
below the surface, the mud and jaws and eyes
of food or death. I want to see my father's father's
hands again, scarred with a life of netting and trapping,
thick gunk of bayou under his fingernails,
staining his cuticles, I want to remember the pride he took
gutting and cleaning what he caught; his were nothing
like the soft hands and clipped fingernails that serve us
in these restaurants cemented in land, the restaurants nothing
like the houses we lived and died in, anchored in water,
trembling with every wind and flood.
And what my father's mother knew:
how to make alligator tail sweet, how to cut up
muscled squirrel or rabbit, or wild duck,
cook it till it was tender, spice it and mix it all up
with rice that soaked up the spice and the game so that
it all filled your mouth, thick and sticky, tasting
like blood and cayenne. And when I see the signs
on the restaurants, Cajun food served here,
it's like a fish knife ripping my belly, and when I see
them all eating the white meat of fat chickens
and market cuts of steak or fish someone else
has caught cooked cajun style, I feel it
again, the word's been stolen, like me,
gutted.

Concrete, Washington

Dewey Patin

Probably the most unusual man I've ever known or known about died Sunday night–Dewey Patin was 98. He was also the toughest, most independent, most self-sufficient and courageous person I've ever known–a legend–for over three quarters of a century.

When my brother and I were teenagers, we told our cousin Doug so many stories about Dewey Patin that he thought we had fabricated this wild man of the Atchafalaya. We finally introduced Doug to Dewey, and Doug was floored. Here was the legendary man he had heard about for so many years and never imagined to be real.

Dewey Patin, when he was 65, jumped on a big buck with a pocket knife because his gun was jammed. On the day I killed my first deer, hunting with my grandfather, Dewey was with us, and he came running through the woods two miles ahead of the hound dogs that were tracking the deer. He burst out into the opening where I was standing and  shouted, "Hey! You got him, boy? OK" Then he took off running again either to find the dogs or scare up some more deer. He and my grandfather, Wade O. Martin, Sr., were friends for life.

I went to his wake today, Tuesday, September 19, 2006, in Breaux Bridge. His son Carol told me that Dewey had been with him on the river Friday, looking for alligators (The season for wild gators is the month of September). His grandson, Fred Laviolette, told me that he went to Dewey's house at 4:30 Saturday morning, having forgotten to call at 4, as he had promised. No problem: Dewey had been up since 2 AM, too excited to sleep. They were going teal duck hunting in the marsh.

Dewey Patin lived a wonderful, focused life, most of it out in the Atchafalaya Basin. He lived to hunt and fish. Imagine a 98-year-old man too excited about a hunting trip to allow for sleep. Many of us would give a lot for that sense of wonder and excitement.

Dewey had knee problems and needed an operation. When he was 90 I was out on the river with him and Carol, hunting gators.

"By the way, Dewey," I said, "You ever got your knees operated?" He seemed surprised that I would ask such a stupid question.

"Mais, when ya t'ink I got time for dat?" he answered.

"You're 90, and you don't have time for an operation?"

"Well, I got the alligator, and then I got the garfish and the cat-fish. I got the deer and the dove and the duck and the squirrel and the goose. Den we got the hoopnets and the lines on the river..." He went through the whole year's cycle of hunting and fishing activities in the swamp and the marsh and on the river. He was right...There was just no time for an operation. Maybe when he got old there would be time.

I visited Dewey many times at his house in St. Martinville. On one of my visits I expressed my disappointment at never having seen him out in the swamp in the beautiful cypress pirogue he had built himself, so that I could get a photo.

"Mais, I got my pirogue right there in the shed," he said. He pulled it out and sat in it , on the lawn, paddle in hand. "Go ahead, boy; get your pictures, he said."

Dewey Patin at home in his pirogue

My brother Jim and I used to drive crew boats as a summer job when we were in highschool and college. One day Jim was coming back from the main channel of the river where a suction dredge was working, and he spied someone in a pirogue near the bank, so he stopped to offer the man a ride and was surprised to meet Dewey Patin, who was paddling from his house on the Whiskey Bay Pilot Channel all the way to Butte La Rose, a distance of about ten miles one way. He needed to buy hardware or shotgun shells or groceries from a store there owned by Mr. Herman Dupuis. Jim gave him a ride to Butte La Rose Landing. Once he made his purchases he was headed back up-river, paddling a loaded pirogue.

Dewey Patin

Herman Dupuis making a hoopnet at age 93

Dewey Patin was a tough man, with perfect posture and a kind heart. He was Cajun to the core, and he will be sorely missed by everyone who knew him.

It is because of people like Dewey Patin that life is good, worth living and sometimes even exciting.

Gifts

by Sheryl St. Germain

--in memory, André St. Germain, 1965-2005

It's Mother's Day, and my family and a few friends are gathered together in my brother's backyard, under the shade of a large magnolia tree, for my brother's gift in honor of the day: ninety pounds of crawfish. Flowers and cards have been given to all the mothers, and now it's time to eat. This is the first time in over twenty years that I've been with my family for this day. I've never tasted my brother's cooking, but I believe in this: the table, holy as an altar, spread with newspapers, and on top, the sloppy orange hill of fat, spicy crawfish, just poured from the pot, still steaming. Cold beer cans ice our hands that are itching to get at the crawfish.

The spring air smells like the only god's breath I ever want to know: cayenne and bay leaf, lemon and celery, black pepper, garlic and onion. A hint of honeysuckle, and the savory swamp scent of crawfish. Their rich orange bodies gleam in the sun like a massed heap of shiny Mardi Gras beads, the cayenne dusting their bodies like pollen, the small potatoes and corn on the cob, the whole heads of garlic, the lemons and oranges, a cornucopia of food, all boiled with the crawfish, all cooked with love and beer and lots of spice, calling out to be eaten. *This is my body. This is my blood.*

Country music blasts from the outside speakers, and those of us who wish to be heard have to shout, but we don't mind because my brother loves country music. My brother is proud and dark and muscled, his shoulders strong as he pours the next sac of squirming crawfish in the vat and stirs it with a wooden spatula as tall as my two-year old niece. I put my face close to the water and bathe in the peppery lemon steam of the vat as if it were the breath of a lover. Crawfish are squirming and dying, their tails curling tighter and tighter into themselves, my brother is stirring and singing along to some song about lost love, my face is almost in the vat now and none of us think this is the least bit unusual. He flexes his muscles—he is a body builder--as he stirs the fifty pounds of crawfish and whispers something in my ear. We must look as if we're conspiring over the boiling crawfish, or getting the latest in crawfish boil facials.

48

Let me know if that asshole messes with you again. *I have no problem showing up at his door and asking if he wants to try to punch on someone his own size.*

Children play with a few left-over crawfish on the grass, trying to get them to grab a leaf with their pincers, or trying to figure out how to make them dance to country music, or how to pick them up without getting pinched. Grown-ups—sisters and brothers, mothers and sons and daughters—sit around the small table eating and talking. We pluck a crawfish from the pile, searching for the fattest and most tender-looking, usually the lighter colored ones, snap the head off in a quick movement, the way you might break the neck of a small suffering bird, quaff the fat juice out of the head like you'd slurp the oyster liquor off a just opened oyster shell, squeeze the fiery tail meat into our open mouths, then reach for another. We kiss the garlic out of their skins, and bite into a potato or piece of corn on the cob that's absorbed so much cayenne our lips quiver with the heat for hours the way they did when our daddy put Tabasco on our tongues for lying, and we must drink many beers to alleviate this wondrous pain. The crawfish still warm, are spiced just right. I have been away from family so long, I had not known my brother to be such a fantastic cook

Piles of discarded shells grow on either side of the table as we eat and eat and drink beer after beer, and our tongues loosen and our voices get louder, and we laugh although there is sadness in all of our lives. Someone has lost a job, but someone's child is graduating from high school. Someone was in jail, but now they're out. Someone's had their driver's license taken away, but their kid's just gotten one. Someone's lost a fiancée, but has a new girlfriend. Someone's son got beat up by a boyfriend, but he's doing okay now.

We talk only a little, about the gone ones, another brother and our father, but it feels as if they're sitting with us, cracking and sucking and drinking and laughing, as if nothing sad had ever happened to this family, as if their ghosts don't sleep with most of us at night, and sometimes seem to strangle us, as if we don't often fear we will become them. Today, the ghosts are eating crawfish and drinking beer.

My mother tells a story about a monk friend she visited who was supposed to be a vegetarian. He'd taken a vow, she says, between cracking crawfish heads, to not eat meat. The monk talked her into taking him to get a bucket of Kentucky Fried Chicken, though, she says, and then hid what was left of it in the monastery's laundry room, for later. She was horrified, she said, at how he set to on the chicken, like a starved man, sucking and licking the bones, as we do the heads of crawfish. *What kind of a monk is that, supposed to be fasting, eats chicken,* my brother demands of my mother. *What are you doing having monk friends anyway?* My mother wipes her hands on a napkin and says the monk was her pen pal for several years. *Pen pal!* My brother yells, full of beer now, *I don't like the way this is sounding.* He's ribbing her, and we all know it. I don't think I've ever seen us all smile so much, together, as if something in the crawfish, and even the beer, and the air, and maybe those gone ghosts, is blessing us with the gift of happiness for an afternoon.

My mother plays the straight man, as usual. But he was a *nice monk, he, he's dead now... and he prayed for our family...* At this my brother leans back in his lawn chair, pulls his cap over his head—you can see the crawfish fat and grit under his nails, and explodes: *He PRAYED for our family? A chicken-eating, supposed to be vegetarian monk PRAYED for our family? That's it, that's why our family's cursed, we finally found the reason. Get the voodoo dolls out, we need to do an exorcism.* We're all doubled over laughing, we smell so much like crawfish, it's in our teeth, our mouths, our hands, our clothes, we might as well be crawfish.

My brother gets up to stir the second vat one last time, and I go with him to put my face in the steam one last time. I can't get enough of this. My brother looks like my father, has his good looks, his joking sense of humor, his same deep-seated wants, although my brother is a better man than my father was. You know, he says, stirring the crawfish hard, making sure they're all done, *I remember one time when I was little, maybe ten, I was runnin' around outside. See this?* he points to the crawfish. *When they sink to the bottom you know they're done.* He takes a swig of his beer. *Anyway, it was really hot, you know how it gets in July, and when I told Daddy how hot I was he gave me a beer. A Dixie.* He looks at me, his dark eyes full of my father, our other brother, and parts of him I hope to know one day. *It was so cold, so cold, Sherry, and it tasted so good, almost sweet. I can taste it still, today. I never forgot.*

Later, my brother stands in our yard, as our father had so many years ago, naked to the waist, his chest glistening with sweat, also as our father's had so many years ago, a black oyster glove protecting his left hand, which holds the oyster, hidden in its full shell that's big as a human heart. His right hand tightens around the oyster knife.

You put it right here, Sherry, in this round groove, that's the eye. And also as our father had, he sticks the stubby blade in, once, failing, then again, chipping the shell, then twists the knife and forces the lips of the oyster open. I admire the strength of his hands, the muscles of his forearms. It is no easy thing to open an oyster. I have tried several times, and each time failed, emerging with cut fingers instead of a naked oyster. I do not have the strength it takes, I have decided, to open an oyster.

Now the oyster is revealed, cradled in the cup of its half shell, a plump and gray glistening like a large shimmering gem, awash in its sweet, holy liquor, and we admire it for a second, my brother and I, this amazing living creature one of us is going to eat. We agree that pearls are nothing, the oyster's body itself is the real jewel.

Still, my brother looks at me as if to cool my reverie, and says, you know what oysters are, don't you? *They're filters, it's not something you want to think about too much.*

What I do think of when he says *these are livers*, filters for the human body, filters that tend to go bad in our family because of what we do to our bodies. Weak livers killed our father and other brother, and mine is so wounded I have had to be vaccinated against the kind of Hepatitis you can get eating a bad oyster.

He slips the knife under the oyster's body and cuts the stalk to separate it from its shell but, unlike our father, he doesn't spear it and offer it to me off the tip of the knife, so the knife won't cut my tongue this time, as it did that first time so long ago, so that for a long time afterwards, whenever I slid the delicious thing down my throat I thought there was supposed to be an aftertaste of blood. No, my brother is more careful than our father was with his children. He gives the oyster in the shell to me, and keeps the knife.

51

They're fresh, Sherry, right off the boat, the guy hadn't even had time to clean them, had to clean them myself.

Suddenly I remember it's Sunday, and I think how much better this is than going to Mass, I think how it's almost like I'm getting ready to go to communion, that's how I feel, except I know the oyster will taste way better than the communion wafer. Sunlight falls softly but fully on both of us, like a ray from heaven, and as my brother reaches into the ice chest to get another oyster, I put the shell of the one he's given me to my mouth like a cup and drink, letting the oyster slide into me with its juice, which runs out of the corners of my mouth and down my throat, wetting my shirt, no crackers or beer to wash it down, just the oyster, whole and sweet and salty, tasting like the brackish waters of the Gulf.

I close my eyes, and see my father giving me my first one, and I think of every oyster I've had since then, I think of my grandmother's oyster spaghetti, my mother's oyster dressing and oyster soup, my sister's oyster and sausage gumbo, my brother's raw oysters, grilled oysters, I think of the most fantastic fried oyster poboy I ever had at a fish place called Salvos, of the way the oysters were so crunchy and spicy on the outside, like the crust of Popeye's fried chicken, and hot and barely cooked inside, just firm enough but still soft, how the oysters, the shredded lettuce and tomatoes and lemon and Tabasco and mayo and ketchup and French bread came together in my mouth, an ecstatic experience like almost nothing else in the world except eating this raw oyster on this gentle spring day given to me by my brother, who spent the first part of his life trying to become the man who was our father and the second part trying to unbecome the man who was our father, and I think of how proud I

am of him, and it's all there as I swallow this oyster: the first oyster, the first opening, the first swallowing, the first time we would take a chance, the first time we opened our mouths for our father, trusting that he would put something good, something truly good, on our tongues.

Wilvin Hayes and 201 lb alligator gar
- Henderson, Louisiana

From the past in St.
Martinville, Louisiana

Seal crossing in Oregon

A few years ago I wrote a song with this title.

Rough, narrow, steep, winding, dirt road NEXT 5 MILES

Washington

Oregon

Washington state

And you thought we have it tough along the Gulf.

Drivers choice? Butte LaRose pontoon bridge

No **diving** from bridge?

It's **Shiners**

Evidence of a time warp at T-Sue's Bakery in Henderson, Louisiana

Can you find the scenic byways sign?

If you need a stop sign to avoid driving into the Gulf of Mexico, maybe you shouldn't be driving.

Many years ago my old friend and mentor Patricia Rickels was a graduate student at LSU. Living next to Pat and her husband was a Cajun couple with a 6-8-month-old baby. Pat noticed one day that the bottle the baby was taking had a brown liquid in it, rather than milk, and the mother would shake it up every few minutes.

"What's in the bottle and why do you keep shaking it?" Pat asked.

"Well, it's gumbo," the mother said. "I strained it, but I have to shake it because all the pepper settles in the bottom." It was then that Pat, who was not from Louisiana, realized clearly that she was in another country.

A sure sign of a real Cajun - outboard motor hanging from an oak tree in the driveway.

Bay St. Louis, Mississippi before Katrina - my favorite sign

PLEASE TRY NOT TO BLOCK INTERSECTION

57

Signs I'd Like to See
Illustration by Ben Blanchard

Naming Hurricanes

I have a friend from the Netherlands, Teake, who suggested that hurricanes should be named after corporations, especially multinationals, rather than using people names.

It's not a bad idea.

Think how many times you've heard the names Katrina and Rita in the last year or so. Thousands--hundreds of thousands. What if you had been hearing McDonald's, or Exxon, or Dell Computers? "Hurricane Dell, a category 5 storm, is bearing down on New Orleans, carrying winds of 160 miles per hour, etc." Talk about a household word! The publicity value would be incalculable.

In order to qualify to have a hurricane named after one of them, corporations would have to bid for the contract. It would be a big gamble, of course, because hurricanes are named early, and any particular storm might fizzle and lose its publicity value, like a commercial in the second half of a lopsided Super Bowl, but that's a chance the corporations would have to take. In any case, the money paid for this contract would go directly into hurricane relief, and the corporation would be required to provide all kinds of additional assistance to damaged areas and people, should the storm hit.

Besides that, imagine what it would have done for Burger King's image, for example, if the company had hired several helicopters and lowered thousands of hamburgers, cheeseburgers, fried chicken, and BK fish sandwiches down to the starving multitudes at the Superdome and the Convention Center in New Orleans. They would have been heroes. Everyone would have wanted to buy fast food from Burger King, to show their appreciation. In no time, they could be selling HurricaneBurgers by the millions. They passed up a great opportunity. They should try it the next time a big storm hits New Orleans. They couldn't lose.

HurricaneBurgers© - 10 million sold

Coastal Erosion

How many of these claims have you heard in the last year?

"Oil companies have dredged hundreds of canals into the fresh water marshes, allowing salt water to kill the grasses that once held the land together."

"It took 5000 years to build up the coastal marshes in South Louisiana and only fifty years to lose them."

"We're losing twenty-five square miles of marshland every year to the Gulf of Mexico."

"New Orleans and other coastal cities are vulnerable to killer hurricanes partly because they don't have the marshes and barrier islands they once had, to weaken the storm surge."

"The sediment that flows down the Mississippi is being wasted. It just goes off the continental shelf into the deep waters of the Gulf."

"We need to get $14 billion to begin work on coastal restoration."

All of those statements are true except, in my opinion, the last one. I believe that the others simply reinforce the futility of spending billions on a lost cause.

Oil Industry Canals in the Louisiana Marsh south of Houma, LA.
Gulf of Mexico in the background

There is not enough sediment in the Mississippi River and the Atchafalaya combined to keep up with natural subsidence of the marshland. It doesn't work out mathematically. When the rivers were un-leveed by man, the land build-up was only three to four square miles annually. That's why it took 5,000 years to add the marshes to the coast. Now a large percentage of the Mississippi River's sediment flows into the Atchafalaya system where most of it settles and clogs up bayous and swamps with sand. A little of it gets out to Atchafalaya Bay south of Morgan City, where it's expected to add about eight square miles of land in twenty years.

But we're losing twenty-five square miles every single year. In twenty years, that's 500 square miles. On top of that, the sea level is rising! Do the math! AND Look what happened to the oyster reefs.

An oyster dredge destroying the remains of a
Louisiana Coastal shell reef, for profit - 1987

I believe that spending billions to try to restore the marshes is a mistake. Also, I think it encourages people and businesses to continue to build and develop in that area. Who will pay for their losses when the land they're developing sinks into the Gulf of Mexico? It **has** to happen. It's a natural process. It can't be stopped.

After the Storm
by Sidney M. Creaghan

Friday afternoon I made a deep,
dark, delicious shrimp stew.
The wind had slowed by then
to the speed of a steam locomotive
billowing slow up a steep hill.
Fog came.
Pushed its thick gray tarpaulin cloth
against my glass doors and windows.
Supple fragrances from my roux
after I added the onions and garlic
leapt out of the big black iron pot
ran across my kitchen counters
sizzled across my tile floors

and slid like a third base runner headin' home
and slammed smack dab into the same glass
windows and doors.
When they met:
fog and fragrance, weather and roux,
at either side of the gray glass
they wept to be together,
sent saucy tears down the panes,
finally puddling on my cypress sills.
By the time I added the parsley and green
        onions
my house had exploded into a bubbling
brown cauldron of books, rice, sassafras
and Otis Redding!

No Straight Lines in Nature–Izuki

Over and over through the years I've heard and read, "There are no straight lines in nature." I've never understood what the statement is meant to convey, nor why people say it or write it. For what it's worth, there are straight lines in nature.

I was discussing the question with my old friend Degas Dugas.

"Well, of course they got straight lines in nature," he said. "Look at all them jet stream up there," and he pointed to the sky. He meant contrails. "What about all them oilfield canal in the Basin?—straight as a arrow!"

"Yeah, but listen, Degas, those don't count. They were made by people."

"So what? They in nature, huh? The sky is nature; the ground is nature; people is nature. You couldn't ax for a straighter line den some of dose jet stream and dose damn pipeline canal."

"OK, D.D.," I said. "I guess you got a point."

Sibon Canal, St. Martin Parish

Washington State trees

I was at the Bayou Benoit landing one day when Degas came in from the swamp with a Suzuki outboard on his aluminum skiff. He backed his Isuzu pickup, with trailer, down into the water in order to drive the boat up onto the trailer. Most fishermen use Yamaha or Mercury outboards.

"Hey, Degas, you seem to like the Japanese makes."

"Damn right," he answered, nodding at both the pick-up and the outboard. "Dose **Izuki** is some of the best, dat's for sure."

June Borel and the Movies

I often work with film companies making TV commercials, documentaries, or feature movies in the Basin, and part of my job often involves finding local Cajuns for small roles.

I had known June Borel all her life, and she was one of the people from my hometown of Catahoula chosen for a small speaking role in "Southern Comfort," a feature film, in 1979.

June was married and had a seven-year-old son, but it became clear that she would not be allowed to participate in this venture without the approval of her grandmother, Ms. Marie, a close friend of my mother. So one day June and I walked over to her grandmother's house, about 50 feet from June's, along with June's older sister, Edith, who would support June in her quest for the big OK.

It wasn't as easy as I had thought. In the first place, Ms. Marie didn't care for Hollywood types. She remembered when a crew making the movie "Evangeline" was there in Catahoula in 1929. "Those people don't have no morals at all," she said. "You can't trust 'em." We didn't argue with that.

"These people seem very nice, though, Ms. Marie," I said. "I don't think you would need to worry."

She wasn't listening to any of that. "And on top of that," she said, "when they got to piss, they just go behind some little bush. They don't hardly hide themselves at all!"

"Grandmommy," Edith said, "you can go anywhere you want in this world-- people got to piss!"

Finally, it was decided that June would be allowed to associate with

64

these crude Hollywood people if I were there every minute to act as her protector. Ms. Marie gave her OK, but it was with great reluctance and many warnings of what to expect.

For real Cajuns, family values still include deep respect for the wisdom and experience of older people, with good reason.

June Borel died of pancreatic cancer in 2003.

June Borel with pet nutria

June feeding a baby nutria

Round-Up

On several occasions I have photographed a Cajun event of a kind that I've never witnessed anywhere but in the Basin. People raise cattle on the higher land along river and bayou banks and into the bottomland hardwood areas. There are no fences, and the cattle become almost as wild as deer. A cattle round-up out there is a major production. Fifteen or twenty horses are transported to the round-up area, usually on a Friday, in groups of 4 or 5, since that's as many as the cattle barge, pushed by an outboard-powered boat, can carry.

A small corral is set up for the horses, and by early Saturday morning, the cowboys have arrived, in boats loaded with steaks and pork chops and sausage and chicken to grill and barbecue, as well as lots of beer in ice chests.

The corral is opened to accept cattle, and a chute leads from the corral to the barge that is tied to the bank. Then the chase begins. Cattle go running in every direction, over the banks, through the swamps, across the bayous, anywhere but to the corral. The last place they want to be is on that little metal barge in the river. The whole thing is wild and dangerous. Steers and bulls attack the riders. Cajun cowboys fall off their horses, everyone is yelling and crashing through the underbrush and swimming the bayous or whatever it takes.

Finally, by late in the day, there are five or six cattle on the barge (sometimes none), and the muddy riders can begin to light their cookfires, start in on their beer and boudin and explain to one another what went wrong or how it took six of them an hour to get one wild cow lassoed and hauled down to the barge.

At first it all seemed to me not worth the effort. All those men, all that danger and work, all day long, just to capture a few head of cattle to take to the auction house. Gradually I came to realize that rounding up cattle was not really the point. The point was to get together out in the Basin, away from civilization, and have good, clean, Cajun fun. The point was not to catch cattle. If all the cattle had been rounded up too easily, there would be no good excuse to go out there again the next weekend and cook and drink and pass a good time chasing wild cattle through the swamps. That is part of what it means to be Cajun.

~

The very best description of this kind of round-up, though it occurs on a cheniere in the Louisiana marsh rather than in the Atchafalaya Basin, is in a book titled *Marshland Brace*, by Chris Segura. I would have to say that the round-up scene is one of the most gripping pieces of writing that I have ever read. The book was published by the LSU Press in 1982 and is probably available at your public library. The main character in the longer story, "Les Perdues," is a Cajun boy growing up in and around Abbeville, Louisiana. It's a great story.   You would enjoy reading it, I promise.

~

Speaking of drinking, that's another thing that some Cajuns do to preserve their identity. I had an interesting exchange with a man in Henderson once, who was upset by the fact that law enforcement people just didn't have any respect for such Cajun traditions as beer drinking. He felt that more leniency should be allowed to Cajuns who were arrested for fighting, drunk driving, disturbing the peace, vehicular homicide, etc., because that was understood to be a characteristic of our culture. We've had a tragic history, and our heavy beer drinking should be accepted, tolerated and understood. (I didn't argue with him; he had been drinking.)

Romulus and Remus

Of all the aspects of traditional Cajun life and work, only one has survived relatively genuine and unchanged, and that is commercial fishing in the Atchafalaya Basin. In a way, it's our last vestige of authenticity.

Cajun music has been adapted and modernized for many years by bands all over the world.

Cajun French is mostly a thing of the past, as fine a language as you could want.

Cajun food has been badly cooked, diluted and faked by "chefs" all over the world. "Cajun-style" food is offered to the public almost anywhere you go today. Even Cajun seasoning mixes are sold as well as imitated everywhere.

Cajun dancing has been tried and learned by people who love to dance, from France, Germany, England, New York to California and everywhere else.

But fishing and crawfishing for a living in the Atchafalaya Basin is the sole domain of one small group, and that group alone—French-speaking Cajuns. Go out there and see, before they've all gone.

There are no black crawfishermen, no Vietnamese or Laotian or Latino crawfishermen in the Basin. And no young people, either. Most of us are reaching an advanced age, considering what a physically demanding livelihood crawfishing is.

Roy and Annie Blanchard at home in Bayou Benoit

For many of us older Cajuns, crawfishing is not simply what we do. It's who we are. It's as much our identity as it is the occupation we have chosen, and the work we have stuck with through good years and bad. Few young people follow their parents and grandparents into crawfishing, though. In fact, none of them do. It's not possible to earn a living in the Basin now, thanks to sedimentation, and poor water quality, and the lack of flow north to south. There are no good years anymore. The last one was 1997.

A good year is one in which a fisherman can catch at least $150 more of crawfish per day than the cost of his bait, outboard and truck fuel and repairs, traps and other equipment, for six months of the year. That's as long as the season lasts, even in a good year.

Roy Albert at the Bayou Benoit Landing, 1983, a good year

I was explaining the situation to my old friend Tooloose Boudreaux recently. Tooloose had graduated from the eighth grade and after a couple of years in the cane fields, he joined the Army, toward the end of the Second World War. Like most Cajuns in the service he became a cook. Cooking is a recognized skill of most Cajun men and boys, or at least it was, when we were growing up

I described the ongoing efforts of crawfishermen, especially the LCPA-West, centered in St. Martin Parish, to get various local, state, and federal agencies and departments to do something to correct the situation, especially the problem of poor water quality in the Basin, so that the people could once again earn a living in traditional ways.

"Years of effort have gone into trying to get help, and we feel that almost nothing has been accomplished," I told Tooloose.

"Well, Rome wasn't built in a day," he said.

"What?!" I replied. "What does that have to do with anything?"

"Just what I said," he said. "Rome wasn't built in a day."

"What do you know about Rome, Tooloose?"

"I know a lot. I cooked over there in Italy during the Second World War. I know that Rome was built by Romulus and Remulus, too, but I learned that in school."

"Remus," I corrected.

"What?" he said.

"It's not Remulus; its Remus. Romulus and Remus."

"No way, José," he said. "Remus was that old black guy who used to write stories about Ber Rabbit and Ber Turtle and Mr. Bluebird on my shoulder."

"That was **Uncle** Remus; he didn't' write the stories; he told the stories. And it's not Ber Rabbit. It's Brér Rabbit. Brér is short for Brother," I added.

"No kidding," he said. "I thought Bro was short for Brother. Anyways, when they finished building Rome, Romulus stood on one side of this kind of low stone wall he had put there to protect the city, and Remulus..."

"Remus," I said...

"Remulus was on the other side of the wall. Well, he up and jumped over the wall with his cane knife out and said, 'So what will you do when your enemy jumps over your silly little wall and comes at you with his cane knife?' and Romulus says, 'I'll hit him in the head with my pipe wrench' or whatever he had in his hand, and he killed his twin brother dead, right there."

"He killed him with a pipe wrench?"

"That or a club or whatever he had available. He didn't mean to."

"Then what happened?" I asked. I had forgotten about the crawfishing problem.

"Well, this pack of wolves that always traveled around with Remulus jumped the fence and just tore Romulus all to pieces."

"That's it?"

"Well, no, they had a big funeral and they decided to name the place Rome, after Romulus."

"Why not name it after Remus?" I asked.

"You mean Remulus..." he corrected.

"Yeah—Remulus."

"I really don't know.... They never taught us that in high school."

"You never went to high school, Tooloose."

"Yeah; well, whatever."

Carol Patin with a replica of the 128 lb. catfish

Foggy sunrise near Bayou Benoit

Language

When I entered the first grade at Catahoula Elementary School, I was the only kid in class who spoke English. That was 1943. My grandfather was an elected public official, and we spoke both English and Cajun French at home. The other kids in Catahoula spoke only Cajun French. I mentioned earlier the punishments applied to school children in those days to prevent them from speaking French on the school grounds. After all, we were Americans, and the textbooks were written in English.

But the most destructive force, as far as language was concerned, was the prevailing attitude among teachers and administrators that the inability to speak standard English implied and conveyed second-class status. People began to be ashamed of speaking French, and the language was gradually abandoned..

The change was so complete that my oldest son, when he attended the same school and sat in the same classroom 25 years later, was the only kid who spoke French. We lived and worked in Virginia when he was learning to speak, and my wife and I spoke to André only in French. We had no TV, and he was four years old before he began to learn English, back in Louisiana. In one generation the language had been essentially lost. French taught in schools here today is standard, not Cajun, French. Cajuns call it "the good French."

Instead of saying "Je vais" (I'm going; or I will go) in Catahoula we say "M'aller courri," or "Mo gans courri." We cut "avec" down to "ec." We aren't "complet" after we eat; we're "plein."

~

An old friend of my mother's stopped to help her on the road near Catahoula. It was a hot day in August and he had just over-eaten. "Mo plein comme un canique," he said. (I'm full as a marble.) When she expressed her extreme gratitude to him for changing her flat tire, he blew it off: "Temps quitte mo la, toe sa jamais a pied." (As long as I'm around, you'll never be on foot). It has become my favorite Cajun expression, just ahead of "Come ahead back!" That's what you yell at someone waiting to back his boat into the water. There was a sign at one of the boat launch ramps at Henderson years ago that read, "50 cents to put." (to put your boat in the water. Now it's about $4.)

Totalloss is a verb to most Cajuns, as in "I totalloss my outboard on that cypress stump under the water."

When buying crawfish bait, we ask for manhattan, L.Y.'s or blue heron, rather than menhaden, ale wives or herring.

~

Speaking of language, I have something else to tell you. I was an English teacher for 13 years, and I went further into debt each year that I continued teaching. At $30,000, I had to quit. I had done my duty. I began picking up driftwood and hauling logs out of the Basin, making cypress furniture, and I started taking pictures. I made a better living selling driftwood to flower shops, plant nurseries and individuals than I had made teaching full-time in college, at USL.

Part of the residue from those years of teaching is my preoccupation (you would call it an obsession) with correct language. Here are a few of the things that bother me:

Lie and lay– Don't go **lay** down on the couch to watch the Superbowl. Go **lie** down. Chickens, ducks, alligators and snakes lay (eggs). People lie. (especially politicians)

Lend and Loan–Don't **loan** me your car. Loan is a noun, as in, I made a loan from the bank. **Lend** me your car. You remember the Beatles? They sang, "Lend me your ears and I'll sing you a song," etc. Remember *Julius Caesar*? Mark Antony said, "Friends, Romans, countrymen, **lend** me your ears." He never said, "**Loan** me your ears," did he?

And I'll tell you something else: Ever since the tsunami hit Southeast Asia, people have been mis-using and over-using the word **epicenter**. Everything is an epicenter now.

"The epicenter of Cajun music is Lafayette."

"New York is the epicenter of the world."

"The epicenter of the insurgency in Iraq is ..."

Listen–Epicenter does not mean center. Center means center. Epicenter is a geologic term referring to the exact location on the surface of the earth under which an earthquake originates. Period.

And then there's "on the ground." Newscasters have gone nuts with that phrase.

"The situation on the ground in Iraq..." Where else would the situation in Iraq be–hovering a few feet above the ground? "On the ground" doesn't mean anything at all. Try listening to a news broadcast or a political interview and see how many times the phrase is used. See if "on the ground" adds anything to your understanding of where they're talking about. They just like to hear themselves talk.

Even when New Orleans was covered with water, Anderson Cooper and others were referring to "the situation on the ground in New Orleans." They couldn't even **see** the ground.

I have listened to hundreds of interviews on National Public Radio, my favorite source of news and information, but every interviewee uses and overuses the word "absolutely." There are other words–exactly, certainly, yes, that's right, etc.–that mean the same thing as absolutely, but no subject of interviews ever uses them.

Everyone says "different than," when they should say "different

from." Only Click and Clack, the Tappit brothers, use flawless English. Listen to "Car Talk" on NPR.

Felix Richard with alligator teeth and boar tusks in Coteau Holmes

Language is sometimes a source of misunderstanding. Words don't always mean the same thing to all people. I was working with a movie crew one day and we were going out into the Basin from the Bayou Benoit Landing. There was a stray dog hanging around, really skinny, and everyone from Hollywood was concerned for its welfare. They decided to take up a collection and give the money to someone who would agree to take care of the poor dog. They raised about $100, and Felix Richard, one of our local boat drivers, agreed to take care of the dog, so he took it home at the end of the day.

The next day, several people went up to Felix.

One of them said, "Hey, Felix, we were wondering how the dog was doing."

"What you mean 'How the dog is doing'?" he asked. "He's not doing nothing. He's dead like a rock. Didn't ya'll told me to take care of him? I took care of him. For a hundred dollars a dog, I'll take care of all the dogs ya'll want."

High water in the Red Eye Swamp

The Ten Commandments
If God She Was a Cajun

1. Don't put not'ing or nobody in front of God. Leave God #1.
2. Don't worship no udder images, like $$$$, flags, or celebrities.
3. When you mad, find another way to say, "God dammit!!!"
4. Stop working on Sunday. You know damn well you need to pass more time with your family. You can't make a living, anyway you work on Sunday.
5. Show respect wit' your mama and your papa. And wit' your kids, too.
6. Don't kill nobody. Is dat clear? Is dere any part of it you don't understand? Well, all right den..
7. Oh, Lord...you knew we was gonna have to deal wit' it sooner or later...**Adultery**. Just don't do it, OK? I wish I could explain it in a way you would understand, but I can't, even if I'm God. Your brain just can't handle it. Don't even t'ink about it. Find something else to do, OK?
8. Don't take nothing dat don't already belong to you, not even one crawfish trap. And don't try to make yourself t'ink you deserve it, or you need it or nothing. Remember, I got my eye on you almost all de time.
9. Don't perjury yourself. Don't lie to make yourself look good. Just stop lying. The same goes for gossip and slander. Stop! And don't say I never warned you.
10. Don't lust after your neighbor's outboard motor or none of his stuff. Dat just makes you want to steal it, and you know what I done told you about stealing, huh?

Listen, my children, this is the realm of the spirit up here. The 72 virgins idea? No way José, you know what I mean? Everybody's a virgin up here, and nobody's a virgin. There's no sex up here--Period. I mean, angels don't have the relevant features. They're virginal but not **vaginal**, if you know what I mean. No matter how many

Americans you blow up, bless their souls, you won't find the kind of virgins you're looking for up here. In fact, you won't be coming up here anyway. Blowing people up is killing, and you remember what I told you about killing, don't you?

And this goes for the rest of you, too. If I let it be known that anyone who breaks the Ten Commandments goes to Hell, and you go ahead and do it anyway, Y'ALL MUST BE CRAZY! Do you know what Hell is like? It isn't pretty, let me tell you. You didn't hear about the Ten C's just yesterday, did you? And I'll tell you something else: No insanity pleas accepted up here, no ignorance of the law, no NOTHING. Think about it, OK, ya'll? While I'm on the subject of being crazy, let me add a couple of new commandments:

11. Don't pollute the earth, the water and the air.

Really, it was a lack of vision on My part to leave dat out. How could I have known dat you would destroy your own planet? Dere are no replacement planets dat I could send you to for a second chance, no. Dis is it, My children. You already cut down almost all the big trees I planted; you turned My rivers and lakes into cesspools. You done "paved Paradise and put up a parking lot," as one of your songs goes. It's time to stop...

12. Don't cheat the poor people of the world. And stop letting dem die of disease and starvation, y'all who have so much more den y'all need. Y'all can do much better.

About 9/11/01

On September 11, 2001, the US experienced a horrible tragedy—a terrorist attack that killed 2,973 people in New York, Washington and Pennsylvania—suddenly and violently.

As terribly sad as that was, and still is, did you know that other people, all over the world, have a 9/11 **every day—times 10?** 20,000 to 30,000 people, mostly children, die of starvation and diseases brought on by starvation and bad drinking water every day, and those deaths are anything but sudden. These people linger and fester in pain and misery for weeks, months, and often years before their bodies give up. That's not counting AIDS.

Many of us remember where we were and what we were doing when America came under attack and nearly 3,000 of us died. Will we remember where we are today and what we're doing? 25,000 are dying **today**...and tomorrow...and the next day...and the next day...

What could our great wealth do to help these people? Who knows? We've never really tried to find out.

I believe that our difficulty in dealing with people in other countries is based in large part on our one-dimensional view of those whose cultural identity and history are different from ours. We don't speak the same language, in many more ways than one.

Practical Cajun Logic

My dad was, for many years, an inspector along the west Atchafalaya levee from our house near Catahoula all the way to Highway 90 near Morgan City. The road atop the levee was dirt and gravel and it was difficult to drive there after wet weather. One day my dad and my mother, who sometimes went along for the ride, came upon an old Cajun couple whom they recognized–Mr. And Mrs Pagniol– walking slowly in the same direction, so my dad stopped and offered them a ride.

The Pagniols thanked him kindly but said that they would prefer to walk, adding that they were in something of a hurry. That didn't make sense to my dad, but he was an accepting man and he went on, thinking, "That's them; they do it their way."

Less than a half mile further, he encountered a huge mud hole taking up the whole surface of the road, and try as he might, he was unable to avoid getting hopelessly stuck.

Within a few minutes, the Pagniols came along, slow and deliberate as ever, shaking their heads from side to side in sympathy, but they went on without stopping. They were not obligated to stay with the stuck car, since they had turned down a ride and were not part of that unfortunate scene. Besides, they were in a hurry. And they had already seen that mudhole.

Was it Aesop or Uncle Remus who spoke about turtles being faster than rabbits in certain circumstances?

~

According to some people, you can't put a dollar value on friendship. Well, maybe.............

My brother Jim has an old friend from Catahoula named Buddy Broussard. Buddy's dad had a bakery in Catahoula long ago, when there was no road within four miles of our house. My dad would milk cows and take two quarts of milk, by boat, to Mr. Halphen Broussard in trade for two loaves of French bread, every other day (Look the other way, IRS).

Anyway, I heard recently that Buddy was raising rabbits for sale, dressed. Jim liked to eat rabbit, and I don't hunt anymore, so I went to see Buddy for a rabbit. He had only one to sell and apologized for the price being **$8**. (It was a big one.) "No problem," I said. "I need that to cook for your old friend Jimmy."

"Oh, Jimmy's gonna eat some of that rabbit?" Buddy asked. "Give me **$7**."

Dry swamp bottom in the Red Eye Swamp

Change

We know how change happens, don't we? We justify or ignore one absurdity or insanity at a time, and we call it change. William Faulkner warned that change, unless it is controlled by wise people, can destroy things that are not only valuable, but irreplaceable.

The more we perform, the more we expose the unique aspects of our culture to satisfy the needs of tourism and commercialism, rather than our own deep-seated, cultural and traditional needs, the more quickly we get lost in the shuffle of change.

There follows part of an opinion piece by Leigh Haynie from the Lafayette *Daily Advertiser*, July 10, 2005, that deals with this problem in an articulate and thoughtful way. Leigh is one of the attorneys working for justice in relation to the fishermen.

> ...The attitude of the powers-that-be towards the crawfishermen—whether that power be a federal employee, state employee, or a newspaper editor— is one of a paternal condescending authority figure. I have been in meetings with the Corps where employees attempted to explain their project to men and women who have lived and breathed the Basin every day of their lives.

> I have listened as men who have never laid eyes on Buffalo Cove explain water flows and siltation patterns to men who have fished these waters for decades. I have heard with my own ears a state employee tell a crawfisherman he has no idea what he's talking about and he should just leave the planning to the real experts. Inevitably, these government employees have a smile on their face, speak slowly as if to children, and sit impassively as a crawfisherman attempts to participate in the conversation.

> And that's the bottom line: no one wants to listen to

the crawfishermen. Every one wants them to be quiet and "know their place." And what is that place? Jody Meche, vice-president of the Louisiana Crawfish Producers Association—West, put it best. In talking about the future of the people, he foresees a time when Cajuns will be relegated to the position of minstrel—asked to sing a song, play an accordion, talk French, cook some crawfish. Put on a show for experts who know best. A Cajun will not make a living being a Cajun; a Cajun will make a living acting the Cajun.

Jody Meche in Henderson, Louisiana

The *Advertiser* touts the benefits of living here. I could not agree with the *Advertiser* more. The food. The music. The arts. The beauty of the area. My family is grateful for the opportunity to be here. What the *Advertiser* seems to forget is that the food, the music, the art, the beauty of an area can only be maintained by people. To ask the very people who created the culture we enjoy to keep quiet about the destruction is not wise; it is insulting. Instead of berating the crawfishermen for speaking, let's include them in the decision-making process. Then, perhaps, we will not relegate the Cajun culture to a museum, but instead it will be a living, thriving, growing culture with a future.

-Leigh Haynie

I don't want to see Cajun Country turn into a synthetic Cajun theme park. I don't want to see our homeland converted into just another roadside attraction. Do you? Will Jody Meche, one of our youngest fishermen, still be a crawfisherman three or four years from today? Probably not, unless someone wakes up and does something about water quality in our fishing grounds.

Let me tell you something about the people who are letting the Atchafalaya die: They have names and addresses and phone numbers. Call them, write to them, send them emails.

I used to defend various state agencies, as well as public officials, when crawfishermen said to me, as they did time and again: "It looks like the people who are supposed to help us are trying to hurt us instead, like they're trying to get rid of us." It didn't make sense to me, so I didn't believe it. How could it be? Why would anyone in a position to help be doing the opposite? Now I say the same thing. Even Sherbin Collette, fisherman and mayor of Henderson, who avoided saying anything like that for years, in spite of mounting evidence, finally said the same thing to me at the end of an interview in Henderson in May, 2006. "It looks like they're trying to hurt us."

Louella and Sherbin
Collette - Henderson,
Louisiana

Who is trying to get rid of the fishermen? The Corps of Engineers that holds back the water and sends us sand? The wealthy owners of the hydroelectric dam at Old River that operates most efficiently when the Mississippi River is high and the Atchafalaya is low? The big landowners who want the water as low as possible

82

because of their mineral and land claims and because land is more valuable to them than water bottoms? The people of Morgan City who have established housing developments in low-lying areas that have to be protected by levees? The crawfish farming industry that profits greatly when there is no competition from the Basin? Politicians with special interest backing? All of the above? I really don't know who's responsible, but it's happening anyway, as surely as the night follows the day.

The Old River Control Structure near Simmsport, Louisiana

The late John Sawhill, former head of the Nature Conservancy, said, "In the end our society will be defined not only by what we create, but by what we refuse to destroy."

Trees and Other Forms of Nature

There was a commercial message on the radio one morning recently that offended me, and I'm not easily offended. One of the huge paper and wood products corporations identified itself as "...caring for the forest." First I chuckled to myself at the lie; then I allowed a little more anger to seep in; now I'm downright incensed. Those companies do not "care" for the forest. They exploit it for every last profit the forest can provide. It isn't a forest anymore, either. It's a tree farm with one single species of tree grown in one particular area. It's planting, fertilizing, harvesting, selling and replanting. I've seen tree farms in the Pacific Northwest and elsewhere. The tree farm owners and boards of directors call them forests, even "future forests." Yes, I know that we are a growing economy and that we need paper and wood products and jobs. Just don't call it "caring for the forest" when the wilderness is destroyed to produce and sell those products.

Clearcut forest in Washington, 2006

Until a few years ago, there were two gigantic live oak trees on a little piece of land just off I-10 at Nina (near Henderson). I had photographed those trees and encouraged a friend of mine to buy the land years ago and protect the trees. He wasn't interested. Then one morning I went by and saw that all the enormous branches had been cut off the live oaks; only the massive, denuded trunks remained. I was shocked and saddened, but I should have known.

After a few weeks, new branches began sprouting. I cheered. Then they were chopped off, and the trunks themselves were set on fire again and again until they gave up trying to sprout new life. Finally, the huge trunks were torn from the ground, the area was covered with concrete, and a new gas station/trash food establishment was constructed, bright and busy and ugly. Who's looking out for the human spirit while these things are allowed to happen?

The oaks at Nina in the process of being destroyed

In my book *Atchafalaya Autumn*, I speak of my fear that the Atchafalaya Basin and the surrounding region are gradually being remodeled. It happens everywhere, when the interest in money and development overpowers the love of the natural and beautiful.

There are various movements afoot at this time to consider and eventually bring about a wide range of development plans in and around the Basin. I believe that all persons who love and care about the Atchafalaya, all who find meaning and peace and beauty in the wildness there, myself included, would do well to keep ourselves informed about these proposed developments as they become evident. We need to support them, I believe, only if they can be shown to be non-destructive and restorative to the Atchafalaya, as we know it and as we knew it.

We must come to recognize some right the earth itself has which overrides the plans of individuals or corporations to destroy or develop it, or to "progress" somehow by diminishing it.

Drying boots on Bayou Lafourche at Golden Meadow, Louisiana

Cajun Joke

What's the use of a book about Cajuns without one Cajun joke? Here is one of my favorites. As you know, Cajuns always want to know where you're from, and some of us don't know much about geography outside bayou country.

Placide and Cyprien were having catfish poboys on white bread one day at Marie's Café. Two other men walked in and sat down, men who were obviously outsiders (des Americains, Placide and Cyprien figured).

"Cyprien, "Placide said, "Go and ax dose guys where dey're from."

Cyprien walked over to the table where the others were sitting.

"Hey, my name is Cyprien," he said and smiled. "Where you guys are from, hein?"

One looked at him and said, "Winnipegmanitoba." The other one said, "Saskatoonsaskatchewan."
Cyprien said, "OK, **tanks**" and walked back to his table.

"Well, Cyprien," Placide said. "What you found out, hein? Where dose guys are from?"

"You know, Placide, I didn't found out nothing. Dose poor guys can't even speak English."

Cypress trees and logs near Bayou Benoit

Shrimp nets at Grand Isle, Louisiana

The Crazy Side of Life

A few years ago bottled drinking water sold by the gallon was more expensive than gasoline. In small bottles water sold at filling stations is still more expensive than gasoline. My guess is that we will be going to war over water some day.

Gasoline prices in Lafayette, LA, in the mid-90's

~

We had a vice-president once who couldn't spell *potato* and who tried to say, "The mind is a terrible thing to waste." What he said instead... "What a waste it is to lose one's mind. Or not to have a mind is very wasteful. How true that is!" -- Dan Quayle

~

Women did not have the right to vote until 1920.

~

Professional athletes are paid many, many times more than university professors and other people who contribute significantly to our society. Coaches are, too.

~

A small company, run by a man and his wife, has succceeded in selling nearly ten million dollars worth of lots on the moon.

~

We buy products endorsed by celebrities even when we know that those people probably don't use those products.

Tim Russert, on "Meet the Press," September 10, 2006, asked Vice-President Richard Cheney about the U.S. having gone to war in Iraq:

Cheney said, "It was the right thing to do, and if we had it to do over again, we'd do exactly the same thing."

~

In mid-September, 2006, Rush Limbaugh called someone else "arrogant and narcissistic," on his mid-day radio show.

~

At a news conference on April 13, 2004, *Time* magazine reporter John Dickerson asked this question of President George W. Bush: "After 9/11, what would your biggest mistake be, would you say, and what lessons have you learned from it?"

The President answered: "Hmmmm...[silence]....wish you would have given me this written question ahead of time, so I could plan for it. [laughter.]   Uh....[silence]....John....I'm sure historians will look back and say, gosh [Do historians say "gosh"?] he could have done it better this way, or that way......Uh......[long silence]............................ You know, I just......[silence]............I'm sure something will pop into my head here in the midst of this press conference with all the pressure of trying to come up with an answer, but.........it hadn't yet. I, uh......[silence]............."

...and a Bit of Sanity

Chief Joseph, when asked about his dealings with the U.S. government: "I am tired of talk that comes to nothing. It makes my heart sick when I remember all the good words and all the broken promises...It does not require many words to speak the truth."

"Good words do not last long unless they amount to something. Words do not pay for my dead people. They do not pay for my homeland, now overrun by white men. They do not protect my father's grave. Good words cannot give me back my children..."

Cypress stump -- the Louisiana state tree

Maintaining Traditions

What is the significance of inheritance? When inheritance is in the form of money or property or investments, we think of it as important, even essential to "life." When the inheritance is in the form of culture, traditions or lifestyle, it isn't so clearly important or essential. We tend to ignore it, not take it seriously. It's more abstract and not so real or relevant.

We seem far more willing to give up our cultural inheritance than our financial well being. That choice would be clear for most people, even most Cajuns. We would prefer to inherit money than a strong cultural identity. This was not always true for Cajuns. So we became financially stable and secure, in a way that our ancestors never enjoyed in France, Eastern Canada or in their first 150 years in South Louisiana. And we became more culturally unstable year after year.

I believe it is in our relationship to the Atchafalaya that we can find our only refuge, as far as our genuine cultural identity goes. And the Atchafalaya is degenerating under tons of sediment, poor water quality, and the lack of helpful attention.

All Louisiana school children know about Lewis and Clark. How many know about Atchafalaya Station, Bayou Chene and the history of the Atchafalaya Basin, including the trading boats, the school boats, the cypress lumber industry, houseboat life and all the rest?

Certain middle and high school students in Ithaca, NY, area know more about Cajun culture and traditions than students in South Louisiana, because I go there every year and conduct slide lectures on scenery, wildlife and commercial fishing in the Atchafalaya Basin and on other Cajun activities and ways. By the time I get there, all the students have read my little novel, *The Land of Dead Giants,* and they have hundreds of questions about Cajuns.

Students and teachers pitch in and we make crawfish stew for all of them. Al Berard and The Basin Brothers Band visited the school one year while I was there, to demonstrate Cajun music and speak of Cajun life. Faron Serrette, one of the band members and a traditional pirogue maker, worked with shop teachers and students, showing them how to make a Cajun pirogue.

Why does this kind of thing happen in New York State and not in Louisiana? Why doesn't Louisiana--with our great wealth in the form of oil and gas, seafood, mild climate, rich agricultural soils, the chemical industry, the Mississippi River and income from tourism-have some of the best schools and libraries, as well as other public facilities, in this country? Ask your elected public officials for a logical explanation. You think corruption in government ended when Edwin Edwards went to jail? No way.

Gambling and Government in Baton Rouge

Rocky Mountain Video

Children spend too much time in front of electronic screens and not enough time in natural surroundings. I have a good friend, Ernie Bernard, who works as a ranger in Rocky Mountain National Park in Colorado. He told me this story, and it illustrates one way in which nature deficit disorder operates:

A family group drove up and parked at a particularly spectacular scenic overlook. A man jumped out of his enormous SUV, video camera in hand, and immediately began filming everything of interest to him, including a small herd of elk grazing in the valley below. Several children in the rear seats started untangling themselves from their electronic games and other activities and began pouring out of the car, along with a woman who was apparently their mother. The man rushed back and drove them all back into the SUV, filming over... "No, no," he said. "Get back in there! You can all watch the video when we get home."

Score one touchdown for electronic gadgetry, one setback for the relationship between children and nature.

Crawfish boil at the home of Roy and Annie Blanchard, Bayou Beniot

Alligator snapping turtle weighing 155 pounds, caught on a catfish
line by Captain Cleve Bergeron, Lake Dauterive, Louisiana

Why not try the road less traveled?
It could make all the difference.

~

{Posters available}

I believe that every true Cajun dreams of returning to a life in the big woods, close to a bayou or river or swamp, growing his/her own vegetables and fruit, catching and hunting for his/her fish and meat, leaving the stress of city/suburban life behind, with all its conveniences, comforts, and hassles.

Several years ago I asked my neighbor Errol Verret if he ever thought of moving out into the Atchafalaya Basin. "Every day," he answered.

Months ago, when Roy Blanchard expressed a version of that dream to me, but putting it off for three years, Annie jumped out of her chair and went up to him, pleading, "Let's go, Babe. Let's do it now!"